BRAND IDENTITY BREAKTHROUGH

Gregory Diehl is the author of multiple bestselling books on identity development for businesses and individuals. He is also the founder of Identity Publications, an organization that produces and publishes books containing ideas that matter. Diehl has travelled to more than 50 countries, enjoys homesteading in Ecuador and Armenia, and kidnaps felines from streets around the world.

Email Gregory:
contact@gregorydiehl.net
gregory@identitypublications.com

BRAND IDENTITY BREAKTHROUGH

How to **Craft** Your **Company's Unique Story** to **Make** Your **Products** Irresistible

GREGORY V. DIEHL

RUPA

Published by
Rupa Publications India Pvt. Ltd 2019
7/16, Ansari Road, Daryaganj
New Delhi 110002

Sales centres:
Allahabad Bengaluru Chennai
Hyderabad Jaipur Kathmandu
Kolkata Mumbai

This edition published by special arrangement with Identity Publications

ISBN: 978-93-5333-470-3

First impression 2019

10 9 8 7 6 5 4 3 2 1

Printed at Nutech Print Services, Faridabad

Dedicated to the woman who scammed me for $5,000 during the preparation of this book. She inadvertently set me on the path of authorship and allowed me to demonstrate to the world that there is no bad situation that cannot be made good through the filter of a purposeful mind.

Contents

Foreword

By Kyle Gray

It was a normal day of crafting stories for a few clients in one of the coffee shops I frequent. An elderly man, probably in his 80s, slowly moseyed into the shop with his bike and a large book. He ordered a drink and sat down to read.

My initial reaction was admiration for this man. Anyone in their 80s, still riding bikes and staying active in their community seems like someone worth learning a lesson from. I diverted my attention away from him for the time being and continued with my writing.

Eventually, I got into a conversation with some other patrons of the shop about the nature of what I was working on. The elderly cyclist, overhearing me mention that I was a writer, seemed to adopt a look of interest and admiration that mirrored my initial impression of him. Perhaps, he was impressed that someone in only their late twenties was engaged in such meaningful work.

When my work was done, I started to pack up to leave. He approached me and said, 'I heard you say that you are a writer. What do you write about?'

He was, at best, disappointed with my response.

I told him that I write about businesses, marketing and entrepreneurship, and I had a book that taught people how to use storytelling as a tool to grow their businesses.

Aghast at the idea, he launched into a surprising rant on why I should be writing about spirituality, poetry, or something else of real worth.

'You're not a brand. You're a human being, goddammit!'

Stunned by this conversation, I was unprepared to respond in any meaningful way.

I tried to brush this unexpected conversation off through the rest of the day. I could have just written it off as one of the many 'haters' I would inevitably encounter on my journey of entrepreneurship, but it kept resurfacing in my mind.

Since that encounter with the disgruntled old man in the coffee shop, I've come to realize that many people share the same misunderstanding of what a brand really is.

For most people, a brand starts and ends with a nice looking logo for your business card. Some people go as far as thinking about a colour palette and some fonts. While these are indeed a small part of what a brand could be, there's a much deeper concept that most people (including my old friend in the coffee shop) really miss. A brand is a way to communicate important and immense value.

Communicating your value is difficult. Many brilliant people have great ideas and talents that have the potential to make a huge impact, but they largely go unnoticed by the world. You can't expect people to instantly understand why you offer the ideal solution to their problems. You also can't expect them to put in the time and effort to study you and figure the truth out for themselves. They don't have the time, so you usually only have a moment of attention to show why and how you're valuable.

In a world of endless noise, global competition, and unlimited information, people are overwhelmed by choices. There are more content and products out there than anyone could even learn about, much less consume in one lifetime. But with this kind of abundance, there's also new scarcity. What's most valuable now are trust and attention. People give their trust and attention to the people or brands they feel a human connection with.

To win that trust, you don't need to be the best at everything, have the lowest prices, or maintain the most expensive website. You need something unique that creates a special feeling inside the hearts of a small group of people you can best serve. A brand is understanding exactly what this is and communicating it in everything you create and do.

You won't be alone in building your business. The impact of your brand will extend beyond how you interact with and engage your audience and customers. It will also determine who you attract as allies, team members, collaborators, and partners in this journey. A clear brand will guide you to people who resonate with who you are and help you on your path. It will connect with something bigger than yourself that others can get behind and believe in.

Business relationships will unfold in ways you can't anticipate, much less intentionally create. A conversation over coffee could lead to a new investor for your business. Responding to a quick email could lead to you finding that key team member you've been looking for. Though you can't predict how these things will happen, clarity on your brand will attract the best possible people.

But a brand goes beyond even the relationships you maintain with your customers and collaborators. It's an internal compass for yourself. The world of entrepreneurship is complex, frustrating and uncertain. You're almost always faced with multiple tough choices with no right answer. You don't have the time or resources to gather all the information and weigh all your options enough to make a good decision. Your brand, clearly outlining who you are, why you're different, and who you serve, provides the framework to navigate these uncharted and ever-changing seas. It's a difficult process that requires constant change, discomfort and self-reflection.

At the other end of the noise and uncertainty is your best self. It's clarity on who you really want to be and who you can really impact with your gifts. It's a source of energy to get you out of bed when you don't want to, and to persevere when times are difficult. It's what will drive you to become a little bit better every day, so you can better serve your audience. It's your sense of purpose and deep meaning in this life.

If I could go back to that awkward moment in the coffee shop with that old man, I would have a response for him—Your brand is the story you are remembered for and how you shared your gifts. It's the sum of the decisions and impact you make. It's the interplay of how people perceive that impact and how they relate to it.

You're probably thinking, 'Ok great, but I'm still not really clear about what a brand is or how to create one.' I get it… I've been there too, and it took years of asking deep questions, making mistakes, and learning lessons to surpass it.

I won't lie. It's not an easy process to figure out your brand. However, it is not only worth every bit of effort, but essential to your success.

Maybe you're just starting on your entrepreneurial journey, waiting for that 'perfect' business idea that will finally get you on your feet. This book will help you find the treasures inside yourself and show you how to use them best.

Maybe you're already doing what you love. You've got something great to offer, but you can't seem to catch a real break. You're trapped in feast and famine cycles (maybe mostly famine) and might even be on the edge of giving up.

Or perhaps you're already successful in the eyes of others. You're making good money, but your work feels hollow to you. You crave moving toward something more substantial so you can feel emotionally aligned with the work you do.

Whatever your situation with your brand identity is, know that you've come to the right place. You're asking the right questions and reading the right book.

In *Brand Identity Breakthrough*, Gregory Diehl is going to help you through the challenging process of deep self-reflection that is necessary to create a memorable and timeless brand identity. Though a series of charming stories and deliberate questions, he will show you how to pick up on the clues from your past and present that point toward the authentic brand you have been looking for.

Gregory has a unique talent for finding the hidden gems of value in people. At first glance, you might find him to be a story of 'odd duck.' He travels between countries like Armenia and Ecuador, places that most people would never consider visiting. He adopts stray cats, and finds homes for them with unconventional cold sales tactics (you'll see what I'm talking about on page 108). He cares deeply about the meaning of stories (especially those that centre around archetypes and superheroes) and breaks down the deeper meaning in them that most of us miss by gawking at their flashy appearances. He is always honest with his opinions, especially when they are uncomfortable to hear or likely to upset others.

None of these things in themselves are hallmarks of a branding genius, but together they add up to someone who is deeply and wholly 'with themselves.' He marches to the beat of his own drum and lives the example of everything he teaches in this book.

By reading this book and following the processes he outlines, you'll also find your own rhythm to life. You'll learn who you are meant to be and how to channel that to make a big impact on this world. I believe it's your duty and imperative to do so, as it is the best way to solve the human resources crisis we currently face.

The 'human resources crisis' was a term I heard first from Ken Robinson. He mentioned the 'natural resources crisis,' something we're all familiar with (e.g., climate change, mass extinction, increased natural disasters, and so on…). The basic idea is that we don't use our natural resources well, hurting ourselves and our environment as a result. Well, the same thing applies to how we use the assets of people. I see the human resources crisis as an equally dangerous situation for our species if we do not learn to correct our behaviour.

Imagine if Einstein, Da Vinci, Malala, or any other great individuals in history played it safe and never stepped into their genius. What if instead of sharing their brilliance with the world, they suppressed it in exchange for a comfortable life? How would the world be different today if that happened with just any single one of them?

I believe it's happening. I believe there are dormant geniuses worldwide with solutions to every problem we face in the world. But they have not found the clarity, courage or desire to connect with that genius. How much brilliance and potential is being wasted every day? What are we missing out on?

So, it's my humble request that you do your part in your small way to discover the genius inside you and serve your highest purpose. Commit to this book and commit to Gregory's process. I promise you, you will be well-rewarded. I'm excited to see how you use it to spread your message and change the world.

Kyle Gray
www.thestoryengine.co
Author of *The Story Engine: An Entrepreneur's Guide to Content Strategy and Brand Storytelling without Spending All Day Writing*

Preface

Many business owners and entrepreneurs today don't understand the essence of what it is that makes their ideas amazing. They lack both a narrative and deeper meaning to their business. They obsess over the most visible components of their brand but ignore character and core values. Without these things, they will never reach the market appeal and penetration their products and services are capable of.

I wrote *Brand Identity Breakthrough* to help current and prospective business owners to craft valuable identities and tell their stories to the world. From day one, until long into the future, these strategies will continue to maximize your impact on the market. A comprehensive brand identity will save you countless missteps along the path to success. It can be the linchpin to marketplace dominance.

Any business or independent entrepreneur has the potential to stand out distinctly from their competition. If you personalize your approach, you can eliminate the side-by-side comparison buyers intuitively make with other businesses in your industry, and occupy a category all for your own. You won't just be the best at what you do—you will be the only one who does what you do.

This book is a journey of personal discovery and value creation. Prepare to be asked difficult questions and discover real answers about who you are and what you are trying to accomplish in the world. Prepare to innovate unique solutions for your customers' biggest problems. Prepare to show off the personality and philosophical values that will separate you from the crowd.

Set aside, for a moment, what you think you know will make your business successful. You are on your way to a compelling new identity that will forever change how your business operates in the world.

ENTREPRENEURS LEARNING TO TELL THEIR STORY

To you, the appeal of your product or service is obvious. But your audience doesn't share your feelings. Why don't other people understand your message? Why don't they see the same benefits that are so obvious to you? Talking about what you do can be more difficult than actually doing it, especially if nobody taught you how to focus on the most pressing concerns of your audience. *Brand Identity Breakthrough* will give you the skills to talk about your idea in the most compelling way possible.

START-UPS WHO NEED A FRESH NEW MESSAGE

Where do you turn when your start-ups former strategies stop working? If you don't know why your customers like working with you, you won't know how to optimize your approach. You won't know which actions are moving you closer to or further away from your goals. *Brand Identity Breakthrough* will teach you how to identify what makes your business valuable in the eyes of your audience and turn it into the consistent focal point of all your outreach.

ESTABLISHED BUSINESSES LOOKING TO REBRAND

Bigger goals will require your company to embrace a change in marketing focus. Maybe you've reached a point where your original messaging strategy cannot take you any further. It's time to move the goal posts and expand horizons. Is there a new vertical that you could easily break into if you knew how to reframe your value propositions or personality? *Brand Identity Breakthrough* will teach you how to present your company in line with your higher ambitions.

It is my earnest desire to help you to become the kind of person you always knew you could be in business and in life.

Introduction

Imagine that you are aboard a plane that has crashed on an unpopulated tropical island. You are the sole survivor. As you survey your surroundings and scavenge what you can from the plane wreckage, you find limited supplies to aid you in your survival in this unknown environment—a book of matches, a blanket, a pocket knife, packaged meals and enough material to establish a basic shelter.

Considering how much worse things could have been, you'd be very lucky to start your life of survival in these relatively comfortable conditions. You don't have to put out any fires just yet or tend to any other time-sensitive emergencies. You have the luxury of taking some time to assess your surroundings and think critically about what to do next. Eventually, though, you will need to make a fundamental choice. This choice will determine everything that happens to you from that moment on. It is the choice to play things safe and minimize the potential for loss or to take strategic risks and maximize the potential for improvement.

Are you going to go out there and figure out how to hunt? Or are you just going to sit in your camp and hope somebody rescues you before you run out of supplies? Are you going to learn through trial and error how to fashion a spear so that you can hunt the wild boar? Will you discover how to collect rainwater and seek out sources for hydration? Are you going to experiment with building a stronger shelter to withstand the changing weather?

Or will you play it safe and hide away, rationing whatever dwindling supplies you have in the hopes of lasting as long as possible until some outside force intervenes and saves you from this ugly situation? Do you see yourself as a victim of circumstance, who can only be rescued by someone else with greater fortune? The longer you delay in making this fundamental choice, the more opportunities you will waste.

The daily reality for entrepreneurs is like that survival scenario on the island. You are forced to sink or swim, either to make the most of what you have to work with in your environment or refuse to take action for fear of making your situation worse. The life of your business depends on the actions you take right now.

At times, it can feel like you are grasping at every straw for meagre results, and that you will always have to struggle to get by. If you persist for long enough and learn from your actions, you will eventually become a master of your environment. You will know without hesitation how hard to throw that spear at just the right angle to catch your dinner every night. Your identity will fundamentally change in response to the demands of the context you are in. You will not remain the same person you were before landing on the island if you embrace the process of adaptation.

The man who waits for rescue may indeed be lucky enough to be rescued. There is still a chance that he will live to see the future, but he will do so without having changed himself at all.

He will have no new skills, knowledge, or character development. On the other hand, the man who masters his environment, even if rescued and returned to his earlier environment, will come away a forever changed individual who is ready to adapt once again and master any other environment/s life puts him in. He is capable of performing many functions and holding onto many identities, seamlessly shifting as the situation calls for it.

Maybe you already think that you have a pretty good handle on the business environment you've had to work with so far. Maybe your present level of information and abilities has been enough to sustain your personal brand or small business until now. But circumstances never stay the same for long. To thrive for any length of time, an entrepreneur must be adaptable to the new environments he will eventually find himself in. If nothing ever changes, it simply means he is not growing. In the end, we are all either growing or dying.

Your brand identity is a product of your own development as an entrepreneur. Are you willing to become the kind of person who works towards mastery of his environment? Or are you just going to sit and wait for circumstances to change in your favour? What defines a master of identity is his level of comfort in situations of the unknown. He may not know what he is going to do, but he knows down to his bones that he is damn well capable of figuring it out. An entrepreneur is able to make order from chaos and spontaneously improve his situation by changing himself.

What if, you don't know, whether or not you have the natural personality of an entrepreneur? If you're coming from a traditional salaried employee position, you might not be used to existing in this way. It's natural to feel overwhelmed at the idea of being completely responsible for your own success in business. However, the fact that you are now reading this book speaks volumes more about what kind of potential resides within you, regardless of your past experience.

Many people spend their lives never seeing the furthest extent of their potential, because they never made the choice to break away from the mould that conventional society crafted for them. There are certainly jobs that do require you to adapt, and discover, and change yourself regularly, but most exist within the context of a larger plan that is decided for you by people higher up in the company than yourself.

This book is meant to guide you along the transitional journey from where you are to where you want to be. The only real way to know your limits is just to keep testing yourself. I hope you take that to heart as you read the following chapters and begin to think about how better narrative, communication and identification could launch both your personal life and your brand to new places if you are willing to adapt and thrive (not just survive) in the untamed wilderness that awaits you.

MY UNCONVENTIONAL PATH

For certain types of people, the conventional path will never be a viable option. Even in early childhood, I knew there was something I didn't like about the way that most of the adults around me had structured their lives. I couldn't understand how the majority of them could be happy spending their time working in jobs that had nothing to do with their passions and which barely paid more than enough to cover their basic living expenses. I felt like it was the accepted social norm to give up on dreams, adventure and curiosity so that we could better fit into the role others had already carved out for us. I knew there had to be other ways to exist.

It wouldn't be until I was a little older that I would finally have the power to explore my innate curiosity about the many possible ways a human could live on this planet. On my 18th birthday, I moved out of my parents' house in southern California and lived comfortably in an oversized Ford Econoline van, finishing high school and supporting myself through freelance guitar lessons and other independent means in San Diego.

The lifestyle experiment didn't end there. The level of freedom I experienced during that initial unguided adventure couldn't possibly compare to the perspective that I gained from international travel after high school. I built my profession as I travelled, which forced me to become adaptable and resourceful. It was difficult at times, but my desire to live and make money on my own terms kept me on my chosen path until I could become financially comfortable.

A multicultural lifestyle also showed me that the world was not how I had been told it was supposed to have been. I experienced extreme cognitive dissonance for years as I continued to experience things that contradicted my previous worldview.

Travelling the world on my own terms taught me that human beings make decisions based not on the reality of things, but on the stories that fill their heads about how things are. I'd been told that Latin America was a wholly dangerous and unstable place. Instead, I found there some of the nicest and most functioning communities on earth. I learned, as well, that stories could be used to alter and manipulate the mentality of people for a specific purpose quite easily.

As part of my global journey, I worked as an educator in countries like China, Thailand, Iraq, Italy, and different parts of Latin America. Having this kind of direct exposure to the developing children of so many societies gave me a unique outlook on the many ways in which people are conditioned to think from a very early age. Volunteering in Ghana with the Africa Youth Peace Call Liberty and Entrepreneurship Camp, I helped the young adults and teens, who attended, to learn to see the world through the eyes of an entrepreneur. This meant not just creating value but learning to communicate it to a world that would be very unforgiving of foreign appearances.

The stigmas they will face in future as young entrepreneurs rising out of poverty into a worldwide marketplace, are the same stigmas you will face as you introduce any new product, service, or proposition of value to people who think they already know what they want. Communication is the bridge that breaks down the default barrier others hold towards new ideas, and all that occurs as a function of your compelling brand identity. Education removes the resistance to new ideas that is inherent in each of us.

Shortly after I started my travels, I met a man in his seventies named John A. Pugsley, or Jack to those who knew him. Jack was a very influential writer on free-market economics and his most famous titles include, *The Alpha Strategy: The Ultimate Plan of Financial Self-Defense* and *Common Sense Economics: Your Guide to Financial Independence in the Age of Inflation*. At the time, I felt lost about the role I was going to play in the global human civilization I was gradually becoming more aware of. He was kind enough to spend much of his time mentoring me in the subjects that he understood would help me to make sense of my life.

John Pugsley passed away only two years after I met him, but during those couple of years, I learned a lot through his writings and the time we spent together discussing how large-scale human society did not have to exist as the random chaos I perceived it to be. It was all part of an elaborate order called the marketplace. This was the first functional filter through which I could make sense of the world of exchange. I realized, then, that an entrepreneur was someone who created new processes for producing value and could convince people to make beneficial decisions they hadn't previously known were possible.

Before this pivotal paradigm shift, I had been struggling to understand how the human race could ever progress from its present state of political and economic adolescence. Despite my newfound perspective on human culture, I didn't know what to do with my life or what it meant to play an important role in the human world. I know now that every intentional human action is performed in the pursuit of happiness or in the avoidance of unhappiness. We are all trying to make our own lives better. Everyone else is simultaneously doing the same thing in their own lives the best way they know how.

We all have different ideas about what happiness is and the best way to acquire it. That's where we run into conflict, and it is only with respect to the larger system of free-market exchange that a solution to that conflict becomes obvious. You begin to see the human race, and every way we interact, as a system of mutual happiness pursuit, irrespective of our subjective variations on happiness. It doesn't matter if what you want is completely different than what I want, so long as there is a way for us to interact where we are both getting closer to our respective goals.

When you understand such a simple concept, you will see that money is just a vehicle through which people exchange happiness, and that businesses provide a method for people to do this in a tailored and systematic way.

THE FOCUS OF THIS BOOK

If the role of a business is to be a system of trading one form of value for something of higher value, what implication does this hold for business owners today? How ought they best to go about communicating both the value they offer and their potential to help their audience achieve higher states of happiness than before? The burden falls on entrepreneurs to analyse the value propositions of their business, embodied in each of the products and services they offer.

In the same way, business owners must also identify what type of person is going to see that specific value, because no two people ever evaluate things in exactly the same way. Once you understand these elements, you have to be able to talk about what you do in a way that attracts the right people and makes them think your business can bring them happiness in a way that no other business can.

The skills I gained in education and sales have enabled me to teach entrepreneurs what they can do to communicate with their audience more effectively and, in time, rebuild their entire brand identity from the ground up. It was the experience of helping dozens of businesses from a wide variety of cultural backgrounds and industry niches that inspired me to share what I have learned in this book.

This book has faced some obstacles on its path to publication, but each has taught me valuable lessons about clarifying my own message. I spent countless hours writing in cafes, on planes, and in the back of taxis in more than a dozen countries over the last year to bring this text before you today. Initially, I even hired a woman to help me create the manuscript and reach bestseller status on Amazon. She ended up wasting nine months of my time and $5,000 of my money, with ultimately no book and little else to show for it.

Rather than let that setback stop me from succeeding, I used those negative emotions to galvanize my ambitions for what I wanted the book to be. The realization that it was entirely up to me to make it a success put me back into the 'island survival' mentality, I had come to know so well on my travels. It was time to adapt or die, and the book you are now reading is the result of my efforts.

Throughout history, the best minds with the most valuable inventions have failed because they could not get others to see the worth of their work. It is a fallacy to think that merely making a great product is enough. The saleability of that product is, at least, as important, and often ignored by the technically minded. The principles of this book are meant for the creators of products and services that deliver genuine value to some group of people. I never advocate tricking others into doing something that is not actually in their best interests. Ethical selling is about enabling others to make more informed choices from better options for pursuing their own happiness.

Whether you are a solo practitioner, part of a small team, or a member of something larger, somewhere within the many interesting facts, features, and people that make up your business is a profound story to tell, which will forever change how the world interacts with your brand. You can learn to look at your own company in the same way that an outsider with no previous exposure does.

You won't find any foolproof formula to follow here to get instant success. Instead, you will find a series of principles that make up how consumers view products and the people behind them. You will be given a new framework with which to examine your own business and your plans for introducing your idea to the world. So slow down, philosophize, introspect, and ask yourself the difficult questions which will lead to meaningful answers. You will make something new out of both, yourself and your business.

Now you are ready for greatness, both personally and in business.

SECTION I

WHY IDENTITY MATTERS

Introduction to Why Identity Matters

Your business is a way for people with different subjective preferences to trade one type of value for another. By building a business that can sustainably create value, you put yourself in a position where people will appreciate your existence and be willing to pay to keep you around. Understanding this one simple principle instantly puts any entrepreneur many steps ahead of the many people who never realize that they are in complete control of how much money they make, merely through the creation of greater value.

This is an important foundational premise from which to operate. By focusing first on creating value, you put yourself into a completely different headspace, and all your actions will be different as a result. Too many business owners look at the monetary value of what they are selling or the cost of the service they are offering, without seeing the value that those numbers are supposed to represent. Figures, profit and loss statements, and balance sheets start to float around in their minds and this becomes their entire focus.

Once your mindset becomes 'how do I create value today?' you've already won the largest battle—the battle of your own internal motivation. If you can truly embody this principle in everything that you do as an entrepreneur, you will have already ensured that you will always be producing and earning a living in some way. There will always be people willing to exchange some value back to you for what you do for them.

Living securely in the knowledge that no matter what trials await you in life you will be prepared to handle them is a powerful form of self-mastery. Waking each day and focusing on what kind of value you can create for your audience gives you the confidence that you will never be poor again, and never struggle to survive. Even if all your worldly possessions were to disappear overnight, you would still have the mentality and the knowledge you would need to regain it all quickly and effectively. That is the power of knowing how to make other people happy through targeted value.

As an entrepreneur, value creation will always be your first line of defence against business failure.

SPECIFIC VALUE MAKES YOU STAND OUT

The purpose of this book is to help you learn to see your own value, the value of your business, and the value of your products or services from the perspective of your customers. Only then can you begin to fashion your identity appropriately. If you can train yourself to think like your customers, you can get a much better idea of what value you should be focused on creating.

Think about a product or a service that you feel connected to in some way. The quality offered is paramount, or you wouldn't have purchased it in the first place. But of all the many purchases you make, there are some businesses that you undoubtedly feel more loyal to than others. The strongest source of this heightened sense of loyalty is the feeling that a company has gone out of its way to create a special type of value specifically for you.

Think of your favourite coffee shop that goes a little bit further in service, personality, and menu offerings. While they are competing with much larger companies that have a lot of money to spend on advertising, you still prefer them because they add specific value to the product and the service they offer. They stand out in your mind better than others, and you forge a real relationship with their brand. This results in them being able to stay afloat in a highly competitive environment and, whether they are conscious of it or not, they are improving the lives of the people they encounter in their own unique way.

This value is not another 'add-on' or 'bonus' on top of the basic service. It is something much less tangible that permeates their entire existence.

Many people today still hold on to the idea that business is about greed, it's about tricking people into giving you their hard-earned money, or coercing them into wanting things they don't really need. Or worse, that it's about putting yourself above them, keeping them down while you get richer and richer and they get poorer and poorer. On the contrary, business is about the creation and exchange of ever-increasing amounts of value. It incentivizes innovation in society, and makes life better for all of us, from the very rich to the very poor.

The worst off among us today in developed nations generally have it better than kings of bygone eras, and we have market forces to thank for that. What emperor, with his legion of servants and hordes of warriors, had access to a smartphone or flush toilet? Who among them was safe from invisible viruses, or could heat and light a home easily? And yet, in today's world, these are things we consider standard for all but the most destitute inhabitants of our planet. Business makes life better for everyone by raising the universal standard of living through access to knowledge and technology.

MY LIGHT BULB MOMENT IN CHINA

It took a profound personal experience on one of my travels to begin to understand the emotional power of being able to give people exactly what they want in a very specific way. Years ago, I was having a miserable time teaching in China. I made the decision to leave the country as quickly as possible to get away from the high levels of authoritarian control and conditioning of children that I witnessed. At the time, I saw the entire few months I had spent there as a waste for myself and everyone else involved.

When I told the mother of a young girl, I had recently begun tutoring, of my impending plans to get on a plane and never look back, I was quite shocked when she literally begged me not to go and offered me a blank cheque to stay and teach her children full time.

As it turned out, this family had been searching for years for a native English teacher who was not only a quality language tutor, so that she would grow in her speaking and writing abilities as quickly as possible, but could also emotionally connect with their daughter, so that she would enjoy the process of learning. They were quite eager to leave China themselves and emigrate to the United States, which meant their children would need to have excellent English skills. She confessed to me that she had seen more progress in her daughter in our few short weeks of working together than in several years prior with numerous other language teachers.

That moment was when the light bulb turned on in my head. Instantly, I knew in a very real way how big a difference it made to them to have someone who could provide exactly what they needed instead of something that was just 'close enough.' While English teachers were plentiful in China, there were none that could cater to this family's highly specific goals in the way that I had already demonstrated to them. I ended up staying a few months longer to work with this family directly, and it turned out to be a highly rewarding experience for me, as I was finally seeing the results of the value I was creating. I realized that everyone has something they desperately need, and they will be deeply appreciative of whoever it is that can provide it for them.

It is common to blame a lack of sales on anything and everything external to the actions of entrepreneurs. It could be the weather, or just labelling customers as lazy and ignorant for buying elsewhere. Most of these entrepreneurs will never turn their focus inward to look at how their own actions have allowed for these situations to exist. For things to change, they have to change.

Blaming the customer for lack of sales is proof that the business owner has not created sufficient value around what he or she is doing—or else has not communicated that value in the right way to the right people. Remember that everyone is looking for something. The only reason we ever take any intentional action in the world is to get something we want or get rid of something we don't want. If owners were to approach their business by waking every day and asking, 'How do I create value today?' their company's downfall would not depend on external circumstances.

Because people's values are constantly changing, you can never be completely sure that the specific value you create today will still be relevant tomorrow. Plateaus in your growth are an opportunity to reflect and add further value to your brand identity. What is it that you need to be doing to solve the most pressing needs of your customers? How do you give them what they need most in a unique and compelling way? Your brand identity must become that of the person who is best qualified to make their lives instantly better in a specific way, just as I instantly changed the lives of that Chinese family at a time when there were zero comparable options.

How do you create and communicate new value to your customers on a daily basis?

1

Can You Tell a Good Story?

It took me a long time to accept that merely being good at something was not enough to garner the attention, the respect, or the dollars of other people. The truth is that people's actions are not affected by what is. They are affected by what they can see and how they think it will affect them. So, while the essence of business may be the creation of specific value, you can never expect a business to succeed by virtue of its good ideas alone. It has to be presented in a way that answers the questions people are asking, solves problems they are aware of, and is easily digestible.

This might sound obvious, but think of how many times you've been held back from getting what you wanted in life because people could not see the value you knew you had.

In my early twenties, I struggled to understand why I was considered virtually unemployable in conventional corporate environments. While I did pretty well for myself innovating independent ways to make money—from teaching music lessons locally to helping retirees sell antiques on eBay, to fixing up old violins and flipping them for a profit—I could never seem to stand out as someone worth hiring in a real company with a salaried position.

My own internal logic was flawless to me. I knew that, with all other things being equal, I was a smarter-than-average person. From my point of view, if you assigned a task to me I would quickly figure out whatever pattern would lead to it getting done as efficiently as possible, making the optimal amount of money for myself and whoever had the privilege of adding me to their staff. So why did I continue to see myself passed over for jobs, which were given to people I was sure I could outperform?

It wasn't until I accidentally stumbled upon my first corporate role as a copywriter that I finally put the pieces together and saw the bigger picture of how the hiring process worked. A music student of mine was thoroughly impressed with my teaching skills and my knack for clear verbal communication. In passing, she mentioned that the company she worked for was looking for writers to fill a temporary position as a content creator for their website. Because she personally knew me, she was able to get her foot in the door on my behalf, and after I had passed the standard interview and skill assessment process, the job was mine.

What I gained from those two months working at a desk in a cubicle, surrounded by other desks in other cubicles, was a new perspective on business culture in America. I realized I had not attracted the attention of the world of 'real' jobs because I had not learned how to present my value in a way that matched what they were specifically looking for. Their job description was not 'bright young man who's good at figuring things out and putting down words.' It was a specific series of qualities combined with real working experiences which conformed to their work environment.

The irony is that as soon as I figured out how the corporate world worked, I had gotten over my interest in joining it. As of today, I've helped quite a few people prepare their own résumés and cover letters to match better specific positions they've had their heart set on. I can do this for them because it finally clicked that I needed to talk about the concept of value in a way that fitted with what others were looking for. I finally learned how to answer the questions people were actually asking.

THE IMPORTANCE OF NARRATIVE

Narratives are mental structures that we use to organize information about the world. If you think back to your days in school, your least favourite memories will probably include the times when you had to sit still and learn endless amounts of information by rote in preparation for a test or project. The reason these experiences are dreadful for both children and adults alike is that we are not designed to learn this way. Our brains process stories far better when the information is connected to changing emotional events.

This is why mnemonic devices and memory palaces are valid methods for retaining large amounts of information, or why some people can remember the names of every minor character in the Harry Potter series but struggle to pass their university courses.

I've always enjoyed watching movies, even the really awful ones, because I find it absolutely thrilling to dissect the thought process of the person who has chosen to tell a story in a particular way. A movie offers the viewer a complete story, from beginning to end, and leads you through all the emotional beats of its narrative in two hours or less. You can easily pick up on the overarching themes and the nuances of character development that the director, writer, and all the other people involved were trying to convey through multiple viewings in a very short amount of time.

Even though we all recognize why this format is important for the success of books and movies, we almost never apply it to the story of our own life. When most people talk about their business or their profession, they list features and facts that they consider important to who they are. This is the same trap I fell into as a younger man when I assumed that merely being intelligent or talented would warrant the attention of the people who were in a position to hire me.

> *You'll recognize the same fallacy in nearly every industry.*
> *'I teach Yoga and Pilates.'*
> *'My company manufactures wooden barstools.'*
> *'Our product is a toaster that sings Beatles tunes while it toasts.'*
> *'I help middle-aged married couples have better sex.'*

These kinds of descriptions are the most basic ways to define what you do. They are features about you, not benefits that apply to me. They can communicate value but will only really affect people who already have an active interest in that specific domain—the people who are already asking the specific question you are answering. They will only respond if they already know that they want what you are talking about. If you learn to tell an engaging story about what you do, you will capture the interest of more people, and they will automatically qualify themselves for what you offer as they learn and retain the most important elements.

The greater the benefit that your products offer, the more extreme the state of unhappiness you will be bringing your customers out of when they make the sound decision to do business with your brand. Use those emotions to your advantage. Talk about the trials and obstacles your company helps people to overcome, but learn to do it in a way where your audience can't help but see themselves going through the positive transformation you offer.

The people coming to your yoga class might be looking for greater freedom of motion and the relief of stiffness in life, enabling them to enjoy activities they haven't tried in years. Maybe your wooden barstools contribute to a unique atmosphere that completely changes the feel of a room. The story never goes only as deep as the technical functions your company fulfils. You can't be afraid to probe a little deeper.

A good narrative is designed to tap into the natural curiosity and emotional engagement that everybody has within them. It is the exact same way that a truly captivating movie, book, or even a song can draw us in from complete indifference to being fully invested in whatever is going on. Characters in our head become just as real as the people we know, even though they exist only as information in our memories. It is a universal tendency for all of us to want to give our minds interesting new ideas to play with and engage our emotions.

Your narrative in business is the story that you should be telling the world about why your business exists and how it can change lives. Part of the purpose of this book is to help you to gradually move away from 'what I do' conversations, and weave an engaging story about the motivation, purpose, personality, methodology, and results that you offer. The more complex the value of your business, the more education a prospect will need to reach a buying decision. This is where good narrative becomes most important to your success.

A high-quality product or service can still sell with only very basic descriptions that lack any real narrative, but every stage of progress will be significantly more difficult. Stories make it easier to draw new people in or convince existing clients to spend more than they otherwise would have. They get people out of their strictly limited practical mindset and into a broader range of imagination, which means opening themselves up to making purchases or other major decisions they might otherwise not consider.

Without a strong company narrative, you will:

- Only appeal to people who respond to very basic or technical explanations of what your company does
- Feel less emotionally engaged in your own business, which will unconsciously limit the effort you put into making it as successful as it could be
- Be overshadowed by competing companies who tell better stories about their strikingly similar products
- Lack direction and long-term goals for your business
- Miss out on valuable networking and partnership opportunities by not appealing to complementary businesses
- Have a weak internal company culture, which fragments the way your team fulfils their responsibilities

However, with a strong narrative, you will incite curiosity in strangers who would otherwise ignore your products. You will have a stronger personal investment in the actions of your company because you will believe in what it stands for and what it does. Your actions will make sense within a larger framework of purpose, which will build upon cumulative progress. The other people who make up your organization will understand the importance of their contributions, and job satisfaction will be higher.

Most importantly, it will be more difficult for current or future competitors to copy your approach because you will have a nuanced combination of differentiating factors.

Keep the following four questions in the back of your mind, as they will allow you to focus on the most compelling aspects of your brand identity:

1. Define your idea—'Why should this exist?'
2. Define your target—'Who needs this specifically?'
3. Define their needs—'Why should they care?'
4. Define yourself—'Why should they buy it from me?'

Section II of this book will cover the groundwork that's needed to hone in on your brand identity, whereas Section III will address the communication training you need to share it with others. Keep going, and soon you will have every tool that you need to tell an amazing story about who you are and the value you provide.

2

When Good Ideas Fail

Business is about creating specific value and subsequently presenting it in a way that others will be inclined to appreciate it. So, why do so many entrepreneurs and creators with good ideas and intentions fail in the marketplace?

As with many things in life, we tend to complicate messaging instead of following the simple, proven principles of success. The premises behind this book are simple enough to understand, and many could even be considered common sense. So, then, why do so many people have such a hard time integrating them as a part of their own business? What fallacies do people hold onto that keep them stuck in the same activities? What patterns of thinking need to change?

Most people tend to follow the path of least resistance, both in business and elsewhere in life. They will perform whatever actions require the least mental strain and physical effort but appear to point in the direction they wish to be moving. This is especially true of the busy entrepreneur who is juggling many different priorities as they seek to get a business off the ground.

Because of the pressure to get everything done, they jump to conclusions without enough thought and consideration. These easy conclusions can end up costing them dearly in the long run.

Despite the many different backgrounds that a professional can have, there are observable patterns among them all which explain a lot about why they aren't as successful as they could be. If they did nothing else but change a few key bad habits, they would achieve a significant improvement in their market position, earn a better place in the minds of their consumers, and watch sales skyrocket without changing a thing about their products.

As you begin your journey toward a more clearly defined brand identity, stop first and take a look back over your own past actions. Now, see if you can already begin to recognize any major errors that you may be committing. After all, success is merely a matter of doing more of the right things and fewer of the wrong things.

USING INAPPROPRIATE COMMUNICATION CHANNELS AND ADVERTISING STRATEGIES

Not all forms of communication are equally valid. The paths you choose must be appropriate for your strengths, knowledge and industry.

Some people are very good direct communicators and, therefore, their sales strategies should be based on having as many direct conversations with qualified buyers as often as possible. This also depends on whether the nature of what you are selling is highly personal or bespoke. Tailored services are difficult to commoditize or sell far and wide with an automated, one-size-fits-all approach. In some situations, potential buyers just need to see a face or hear a voice before being emotionally comfortable enough to make the purchase they might already know they want.

In other cases, the product may be well-suited to marketing through social media or a similar 'mass outreach' channel. If the buyers of that particular product are active on social media and make their decisions based on a company's willingness to engage with them on these platforms, then this is where the emphasis should be placed. Maybe your audience will feel more comfortable giving you their money and building an ongoing relationship if they see daily reminders of your activity in a more casual context. Maybe your products are just better suited for online shopping and impulse purchases.

Whatever the case, you have to understand both your vehicle and the terrain ahead of you before you can plan your journey. Where do the people you want to talk to spend their time and what kind of communication do they respond to? How does that line up with what you know you're best suited to do? What skills or tools must you acquire to better match your strengths and your market's preferences?

Since you can't be expected to be a master of all outlets, it makes sense to start with what you know and either hire or partner with others whose skills complement your own. In this way, each of your actions become supported by the actions of everyone else you work with for greater synergy. My own strength lies predominantly in direct communication and focused articulation. Without the help of others who could help me to present my message in the right context and get it out to the right people, the strength of my message alone would be meaningless for my success.

STAYING IN THE SAFETY OF GENERIC VALUE PROPOSITIONS

Entrepreneurs are often afraid to get very specific in their messaging because they believe it will scare off many potential buyers who don't respond well to that particular way of communicating. This is the 'numbers game' mentality—thinking that the key to success is just getting in front of as many people as possible and waiting for the revenue to start flowing in.

But it is vital for small businesses that cater to niche demands to communicate in a way that a small group of people will find highly attractive, even if others will ignore it or even be outright offended by the content. The only opinions you need to worry about are those of your target market. In other words, the people who are qualified to actually purchase what you are selling. Even the negative responses from those who would not be your buyers can actually have a net positive result on the growth of your brand because they call attention to your existence. The aim is to focus on attracting those that have a definite interest in buying your specific services.

The upside to getting specific is that people are willing to pay more for something that looks different, rare and special than something that looks like it was made for everyone. You have to understand that if everyone wanted exactly the same things all the time, commerce would be impossible. We would have no incentive to exchange whatever we currently have with someone else who has something we want more. So, focus on designing products and services that meet a very specific and deep demand, and on crafting the message that speaks directly to the people who most want what you offer.

Remember that it doesn't matter if you scare away 99.99 per cent of people, so long as you are attracting the right 0.01 per cent who matter. Here are the generic value phrases you can begin to eliminate from your marketing vernacular immediately:

'100 per cent satisfaction guaranteed!'

'We work harder than our competition.'

'Great value at a low price.'

Always remember that your customers are evaluating whom to choose from. Every company has a set of competitors, and they need to figure out how to look distinct from every other available option. Every dollar spent is competing against every other way that dollar could have been spent. Your task is to figure out how to make it really clear for them how and why you're different.

The ideal situation is when they think of your product as being part of a completely new category offering them something that no one else caters to. This is commonly referred to as having a Unique Selling Proposition (USP) or Unique Value Proposition (UVP) and will be covered in greater detail in **Chapter 6: Developing a Unique Selling Proposition**.

ARBITRARILY CAPPING SUCCESS

Limits are broken in every field of human action with every passing day through superior knowledge and technology. You must be brave enough to test the waters and see how far you can go before resigning yourself to mediocrity. Whatever others have accomplished can give you valuable perspective on what is possible, but it should by no means be taken as irrefutable law.

It doesn't matter how big or successful you think you can grow, the number of people you can sell to, the amount of money you can charge for your services, or even the quantity you can offer. These are all forms of arbitrary limitation. They are usually based on personal tradition or 'common knowledge,' which isn't knowledge at all and not the result of real market experimentation.

This is not to say that there are no limits. There are very real limits to everything in reality. In fact, limits are how we define what is real. The important thing is to identify what is an actual observable limit, based on physical law and market conditions, versus what is an artificial limitation that you've invented in your own mind or inherited from others.

This is the goal of discovery—to determine where real limitations exist and where we have imagined them to be. It is important always to ask questions of yourself and of the market. Why is this a limit? What prevents me from selling more? Where are the new markets where I am not selling at the moment? Who else could benefit from what I offer that currently does not know I exist or see the value in what I do? Everything that is considered known today was arrived at through this exact same process of inquiry, and we are a very long way away from knowing everything.

It applies the same to business as it does to personal goals. If you ask the average person who's starving in their business, someone who is barely making ends meet, how they could generate $1 million in revenue within the next calendar year, they would just be flabbergasted at such a large number because they are used to conceptualizing money in groups of hundreds or thousands at most. They consider it outside the realm of possibility, simply because they do not understand the components of the final product of $1 million dollars in revenue.

Of course, the answer is always the same, no matter how big the number. To make $1 million in revenue, you need to sell $1 million worth of value. This can be done as a single dollar one million times, as 1 million dollars one time, as 1,000 dollars 1,000 times, or anywhere in between. It's not magic, and it's also not rocket science. It's a process that's entirely logical and not terribly difficult to understand. It's just that the concept is overwhelming, compared to where most people are coming from, and they have already accepted that it isn't realistic. They can never begin to formulate a plan that will actually make it happen.

Breaking things down into smaller goals will also help. How will you increase your sales by $10,000 or $100,000? Once you believe that progress can be made, it will be easier to make a plan to achieve these goals. Most people can conceive of what $10,000 looks like, how hard it is to make, and what it can purchase. Therefore, they can begin to align their actions around the idea of it.

IMITATING WITHOUT INNOVATING

You only discover where your real limits are by putting yourself out there, by trying new things, and watching what happens when you go where no one else has gone before. Never feel like you need to adhere to the limitations of conventional thinking or action. The very nature of being an entrepreneur is that you create things which do not yet exist. You are, by definition, unconventional.

Most people don't test themselves because they are terrified of the unknown, of risk, of novelty and of newness. As a result, they copy whatever is already popular. They see that something has been moderately successful for someone else, and so they copy it with no further reasoning than the fact that it seems to be working. Where they fail is that they do not add their own signature—some type of proprietary improvement in style or function—which means they are indistinguishable among established competitors as a result.

Even if they manage to provide the same product in a more efficient way or offer superior quality, they are still limited by the market that has already been captured. They are fighting for their share of a market someone else has created and already retains majority control over it. What they need to be doing is innovating by trying something new that they're not sure will be successful, but which is, at least, partially based on the proven principles of success.

You will see this in movie releases, fashion trends, and all other types of patterns in buying behaviour. Movie studios will copy whatever genre or style of film has been recently popular, so we have all suffered our way through the trend of gritty superhero reboots following the wild success of *The Dark Knight*, or young adult novel adaptations because movies like *Twilight* and *The Hunger Games* did so well.

The people whose job it is to decide which movies are put into production next think that imitating these runaway hits is the key to success. Next year, it will be something different, because someone else has accidentally discovered success with a new thing. You can bet that the copycats will be there to follow closely behind.

This doesn't mean that you can't learn from what other people have proven works and use it to your advantage. What you choose to produce can and should be a mixture of both old and new elements. If you do something that's too new, people have no frame of reference for it. They can't even understand what they're looking at. If you take something that is already accepted and change it just enough that it can be considered distinct and better, you're pushing the limits and giving consumers something they didn't even know they wanted.

A good way to locate that sweet spot of newness is to find a popular product or service on the market which works adequately for most people most of the time but fails to serve specific needs perfectly. People only continue to use a subpar solution if a better alternative doesn't exist. When products exist to serve a very large general audience, the market demands become fragmented into much more specific niches. Anyone can come along and take a generic idea, which has already been proven in the market, and reformulate it to accomplish a more specific purpose.

The failure to implement these principles into fundamentally valuable ideas is why so many entrepreneurs never even get off the ground with new businesses. Or maybe they find a following with a core group of true believers, but never break out into greater adoption. My goal is to set entrepreneurs up for the maximum chance of success from early on in their development, so that good ideas go as far as they deserve to with the value they provide.

The next question I want you to ponder in the following chapter is about your perspective of yourself and your ideas as they apply to your business. Do you really see the value of your company through the same eyes as your target market? Why or why not? The answer to this question will determine the foundations of your new brand identity.

3

Why You Don't See Your Own Value

Branding is taking the image that you hold of yourself or your company and turning it into society's collective vision. This means that for your branding to have the effect you desire, you have to understand what type of identity you are trying to show to the world. This is extremely difficult for most people to do with their own business for several reasons.

ENTREPRENEURS ARE TOO CLOSE TO THEIR OWN BUSINESSES

Most people are much too close to their own business to see their own value clearly, and it seems to get harder and harder to maintain an objective perspective of things the longer they have been in business. When they've been doing things one way for a certain amount of time, and they've had some success with it, entrepreneurs will often get trapped in that particular pattern of thinking. There is a lot of intellectual and emotional inertia which has to be overcome when someone voluntarily changes their mindset. It's the same reason people will usually maintain the same core values they were taught in childhood throughout their lives, unless they intentionally seek to challenge them.

I've known many entrepreneurs whose ideas about why people bought their products turned out to be completely different to the reasons given by the customers themselves. First, the owner gave me the complete rundown of how their business worked, who they thought their market was, or what made them want to buy. Then, after exhaustively polling and consulting, individually, with core members of their audience, I heard a very different story about why they chose to do business there. Their answers ranged from specific practical features of their products to less tangible aspects of trust and emotional intuition.

Sometimes, it was the success of a particular kind of marketing that the competition had failed to capitalize on, such as copious blogging and article writing. Other times, it was merely that their company personality matched more closely the type of professional they found appropriate for that niche. They had unwittingly cornered the market of more positively oriented people by talking about the abundance and rewards that came from working with them, instead of spreading the fear of loss and focusing on the negative aspects of not taking action, as their competitors had.

Most of these companies had just done what came naturally to them, and in doing so, stumbled into a moderate amount of success. When they tried to systemize and scale that success higher though, they had no idea of why their approach worked. Therefore, they couldn't optimize around it. They couldn't build a real identity with it. That's when it became necessary to dissect their own history and figure out what was truly valuable in the eyes of the consumer so that we could turn fortunate happenstance into controllable growth.

ENTREPRENEURS DON'T KNOW HOW TO TALK ABOUT THEMSELVES

Even if you have developed an eye for seeing what makes other people want to buy from you, the odds are that you lack the articulatory powers required to get that information across in a message that is as concise as it is profound.

No matter how passionate you are, or how great your product is, do you know what words I will need to hear in order to immediately see the specific value that will drive me to make a purchasing decision? Do you know how to put sentences together in a way which is both appealing and straight to the point? Maybe your tendency is to ramble on and on or jump the gun well ahead of time and start asking for an order. If you don't understand the point you are trying to reach and how to use words as a bridge to get there, your message will be overlooked and ignored.

Watch the entrepreneurial contestant show *Shark Tank* to see live examples of this. Most of the entrepreneurs who pitch their start-up to investors simply don't know how to explain why their product is a good investment opportunity. Many of these people are extremely clever and have worked very hard on products that hold enormous potential in the marketplace. In those precious few minutes when the spotlight is on and they have to convince venture capitalists why their business is worth risking tens or hundreds of thousands of dollars on, they miss the mark completely.

I once had a call with a woman who had appeared on *Shark*

Tank in one of its earlier seasons and had failed to secure a deal from any of the investors. She was promoting an obscure beauty product with which she had experienced some limited early market success. Despite these initial sales, she bombed horribly in front of the sharks. Although she seemed overwhelmingly enthusiastic about her product, she was completely unprepared to address the concerns that an investor might have.

However, there was no shortage of talk from her about all the things she liked about her own product, and the things that the few people that she'd gotten to try it liked about it. What she had not done was thought enough into the future about the things that an investor would be concerned about. She had little specific knowledge about sales numbers, market size, or even the basic safety of the product. She was just so pumped about how great the product was that she assumed her enthusiasm would be infectious and she would surely leave with a deal from one of the sharks.

The point is she did not think at all about what the potential obstacles might be for somebody who would be giving her hundreds of thousands of dollars to get involved in her company. She could not see the other side's perspective at all. She only saw her own, and that doomed her from the outset.

Had she had the opportunity to be coached and trained before she appeared on the show, her coach could have taken on the role as the investor for her and drilled her over and over with every conceivable problem that could exist with her product or its potential for return on investment. She could have been taught how to talk about it in the ways that would minimize or negate those problems and to latch onto the concerns that an investor would have.

An investor is not the same thing as a consumer. They are buying the business itself, not the end product it produces. They don't care as much necessarily about how wonderful it is to use your product. They're concerned more with whether or not someone else will buy it. Their reasons for talking to you are not the same as a consumer who uses the product. This unfortunate woman made the mistake of trying to stir the emotions in them that would lead to an impulse purchase through momentary excitement alone, and experienced investors simply don't operate that way.

Being a good communicator is about not just speaking to what is said, but also what is not said. It's anticipating what they could say to you and addressing concerns before they are voiced when they might unconsciously be thinking them. It's about asking the right questions which elicit the information you need to present yourself in a way that leads to an informed buying decision they won't regret. If your goal is to learn how to sell yourself better, pay close attention as we enter **Chapter 9: How to Sell Who You Are**.

ENTREPRENEURS ARE UNWILLING TO ADAPT

The marketplace is not static. It is a living, changing ecosystem. When Darwin talked about survival of the fittest, he didn't mean necessarily the strongest, nor the fastest, nor the best at swimming, nor any other specific trait such as these. He meant that the species which adapts best to its environment proliferates. The conditions of the market never stay the same for long, and nor do the needs of your customers.

What people find valuable changes with their day-to-day emotions, the influence of their upbringing, social trends, technological standards, and so much more. Because it is always changing, you too also need to change with it if your goal is to ensure that you always fit the market. A successful business is one that will shift as needed to meet its target market's conception of happiness.

To a degree, it is possible to influence what people want, but you will never be the only major influencing factor in their lives. Things will change in ways that are outside of your control. Even the largest companies in the world, the Coca-Colas, the McDonald's, and the Microsofts, are all subject to the whims of very fickle buyers. Many of the demographics, who were historically their biggest consumers, have changed their buying behaviour. You can't force people to want what you are selling simply because you think it's the cat's meow. The success of your brand comes from participating in an ongoing conversation, not a unilateral edict.

The only constant in human behaviour is the principle of seeking happiness, but subjective definitions of happiness will always be changing. 'Product-market fit' is what occurs when what you're selling lines up flawlessly with what people are seeking to buy. You cannot let your pride and stubbornness keep you locked into an old idea or way of creating value in the world. You also don't have to abandon your own internal desire in your entrepreneurial actions completely. There is always a way to combine your passions and talents with what others want.

In **Chapter 5: Uncovering Your Core Values**, you will learn to tap into the root of what drives your entrepreneurial pursuits, so that you can start to mould them into something that is as attractive to you as it is to the market. There are far too many stories of ostensibly successful business owners who feel trapped running companies that serve only as capital creation machines. They have no inherent interest in what they are producing. There is no personal or spiritual fulfilment in their actions or the impact they are having on the world. It is possible for you to make money while doing what makes you feel most fulfilled, but only if you learn to see your value the way the market does.

Really reflect on what it is that has made your company successful so far. If you are a new or prospective entrepreneur, can you accurately predict the response that other people will have to your idea? Can you tell me specifically what they will like about it, and why they would be willing to choose it over all the other available options in the market? Does it solve a problem that is big enough to be worth solving? You may be surprised to find that with just a few tweaks to your old idea, it is not too hard to create something that becomes irresistible to the right group of people.

In the following chapter, we will shift the focus of value onto your audience so that we can determine what might stop them from seeing something that is truly unique and valuable in your business. You'll realize that it's not enough just to be amazing. The rest of the world has to see how amazing you are and that means the burden falls squarely upon you to make it obvious in all your communications. It's time to share the value you see in yourself with the rest of the world.

4

Why Others Don't See Your Value

Once you start the process of creating a new brand identity, it's easy to get caught up in the pitfalls and traps along the way, which can stop you in your tracks or lead you astray. Learn to recognize them early on, so they can be overcome or avoided entirely. You'll see examples of these pitfalls pop up from time to time in the case studies included in Section IV, but try to reflect upon your own situation as you read and recognize where they may already be plaguing you.

Even if you have conquered the barriers that prevent many entrepreneurs from understanding their own value, a whole new battle awaits you in getting others to see the same thing in you that you readily see in yourself. We are all naturally biased about ourselves. We give ourselves special attention that others do not necessarily do. This is partially because we spend more time in our own company than in that of anyone else and, therefore, have insider knowledge. It is also due to our ego's tendency to place special importance on our own sense of identity, which is a valuable survival mechanism when it's made to serve us.

This chapter will show you how to look through the eyes of the rest of the world, or more specifically, a very precise portion of them that meet the criteria of your target demographic. If you've ever wondered why it was so hard to get through to other people as you tried endlessly to promote your latest project, the information contained here will show you what you've been lacking.

It's not as simple as merely memorizing the right sales pitch or mastering a particular marketing platform. It's about getting out of your own way long enough to look at things from the perspective of a different person and adjusting your words and actions according to the expectations and methods of interpreting reality already present inside them.

If that sounds intimidating, don't worry. It's easier than it sounds, and it's not something you have to learn to do for every single person on Earth. That would be a monumental task indeed. You need only learn to recognize the internal evaluation systems of the people you will be dealing with directly as a part of your sales processes. Their behaviour can then be extrapolated to cover the others who will only indirectly be exposed to your more far-reaching marketing efforts.

So, with that in mind, let's dive into the most common reasons why the people you present yourself to will often fail to see the value you intend for them. This new awareness will form the foundation for the steps you need to communicate effectively with your audience. It will save you countless missteps that stem from false premises about what your audience perceives.

ENTREPRENEURS OVERPROMISE IN BOTH CONTENT AND CHARACTER

Everyone on Earth would like to believe that they are special, which is rather unfortunate, because nobody will ever see you the same way that you see yourself. We are all biased about our own opinions, and that extends to all our ideas, all our possessions, and all our relationships. Everybody unconsciously thinks that their baby is the cutest, their spouse is the most attractive, and their life is the most memorable or most worth talking about.

When you have an idea for a company or a product, you will automatically give it extra credence by virtue of the fact that you are the one who thought of it. You will think it's better than other ideas that share the same characteristics. Other people will not see it in the same light without a significant marketing effort from you. You must be cautious about becoming a zealot for your own creations. Be vigilant about the effect of your own ego on your judgment. Always seek to see things from the point of view of an unbiased other.

Everyone wants to believe that their product is the best thing ever, and that level of confidence certainly plays its role in your entrepreneurial success. While it's vital to have genuine passion and enthusiasm for what you're doing, it comes across as cartoonish unless you are catering to a very specific kind of audience that feels exactly the same way you do. To most people, your claims and particular brand of excitement will be literally unbelievable. Contrary to popular belief, you will immediately turn off a large class of discerning buyers if you come out saying that your thing is the best thing ever.

This is a type of overpromising, and it is the exact opposite of what you should actually be trying to do. There's a very important difference between actually getting someone to reach the conclusion that they're ready to buy your product according to their own internal buying processes, versus creating an emotional spike that momentarily overcomes their better judgment. Emotional peaks wear off very quickly, whereas sound decisions last a long time.

Even if you succeed in getting someone to take out their credit card or hand over their cash, they may realize soon afterward that they didn't actually want what you sold them. It doesn't actually solve the problem they have. They were just so caught in the moment because you made such grandiose promises about what the product was capable of. You've essentially just emotionally bullied them into making a decision that was not actually in their best interest, and you have failed as a purveyor of value.

Entrepreneurs overpromise because they don't know their own value, or they haven't put their message in front of the right type of people. The irony of this approach is that if your product was really everything you thought it was, you wouldn't have to rely on exaggeration and hyperbole. Maybe you just come from an antiquated paradigm of pitching, where everything must be in your face and over the top. You are copying the tactics of what you see other people doing in specific scenarios where success is actually possible, such as the modern infomercial. Or worse, you are following in the footsteps of failures and outright conmen.

Avoiding these bullying sales tactics, which just intimidate people into buying things they don't really need, can become a core part of your company's identity. In a world where everyone is sick of being taken advantage of by the very people they turn to for help, you have the opportunity to stand out as one of a precious few who are genuinely helpful and educative. You will feel infinitely more confident in what you are promoting when you can present it in this way, and you will earn a highly favourable place in the minds of your clients—one which encourages repeat business and word-of-mouth promotion.

Don't misinterpret my words here to mean you shouldn't be enthusiastic or proactive about your business, especially if that's a part of your natural personality. If so, it makes sense that this should extend to your brand personality as well. If it speaks to your audience, you owe it to them to craft a message that will help them to realize how they can improve their own lives with your help. There's a big difference between a natural brand personality and someone who is trying to convince himself that his idea is more valuable than it really is. His overconfidence and unbridled optimism exist only to fulfil the nagging doubts that plague him.

ENTREPRENEURS LACK ENTREPRENEURIAL EMPATHY

The solution to personal bias is always to make sure that the focus of your product does not rest upon you alone. It must always be about whatever your audience is looking for. Because no two people are ever exactly the same in their marketplace evaluation, your perfect solution will never be everyone else's perfect solution. That's okay. By maintaining marketplace empathy, you will gain the perspective to see things from other people's points of view.

Sometimes it's as simple as asking what they want, although what the market claims it wants is not always the same as what it actually does. This is the best approach if you are more intellectual than emotional and lack the intuition to figure out naturally how people will respond. Talk to them. Mentally put yourself in their position to realistically predict their actions. Thought experiments can take you very far, but they must be corroborated by real evidence.

The reason we are so ineffective at this is that we've spent our entire lives never having to think this way. Most people are not used to looking at their actions from the market's perspective, or from a specific group of people's point of view. In this way, entrepreneurship is one of the best teachers of real empathy you could ever ask for.

Return to the island survival analogy we began with for a moment...a good hunter gets to know their prey. A hunter who has adapted to his environment knows where the boars hang out, where and when they go to eat or to sleep, and so on. He knows this so that he can devise the ideal strategy to sustain himself. You don't even need to have ever hunted to reach this state. You just need to be a thoughtful, observant person with the intention of feeding yourself.

If, however, you've spent your entire life having food brought to you, it simply isn't a problem you've ever had to put your mind to solving. You've never had to consider where your next meal is coming from or the best way to acquire it. You take its very existence in your life for granted, and nothing will change until you experience enough discomfort to dislodge you from your present state of being.

Now consider how many aspects of entrepreneurship this remains true for if you've had only conventional salaried job positions all your life. There's an ecosystem built around you, designed explicitly to make it as easy as possible for you to perform the functions of your specific job. You don't have to learn patterns of behaviour or optimize systems for your own betterment. You are simply a cog in an elaborate machine, and the variables you will deal with on a daily basis have been intentionally minimized. Your life is easy because somebody above you has taken on the responsibility of learning the system for you.

If your goal is to be more empathetic and to start to see things from another person's perspective, you must combine intellect with intuition. If you're in a sales conversation with someone, you can open your awareness enough to read their emotions and respond in the right way to them. However, it's impossible for anyone to get into such an emotionally open position with thousands or millions of strangers around the world and intuitively respond to their feelings. This is where critical analysis is useful.

Personally, I don't know anything about sports. I've never intentionally watched a sports game in my entire life. However, if I talk to somebody who gets excited about the Super Bowl, or the next big baseball or soccer game, I can still understand their perspective on why it's interesting and why it's so important that they watch the game with their friends. I can do this even though I don't share any of those same emotional responses. As long as I can understand on an intellectual level why they feel the way they do about the experience, I can still sell to them as sports fans, because I will be speaking to them where they are.

People have to understand that this market empathy is a specialized skill. Most of us aren't naturally good at seeing and feeling things from another person's perspective, but it can be developed through practice and obsession, to the point where it is always working to help you succeed with your customers.

It's a very dynamic process, which is why adaptability is so important.

Many people need to be taught exactly how to talk to specific customers, either to close a sale, resolve a dispute, make them happy enough to avoid granting a refund, or just bypass a scathingly negative review. This involves emotionally navigating potentially volatile situations and reading the emotions of both parties involved in very tense moments to achieve as much peace as possible. It takes an enormous amount of empathy to see things from everyone's perspective and arrive at a solution that will leave everyone walking away from the encounter as satisfied as possible.

Society isn't set up so that people are forced to see things from others' perspectives unless they go into some line of work that necessitates empathizing with others on a regular basis. Good teachers, nurses, and anyone involved in interpersonal work gets this. One reason why great actors are paid so much is that they excel at getting the viewer, a complete stranger, to immediately empathize with them by stirring their emotions in a highly calculated way through their performances. That's why, if a performance is good and a role well written, we actually care what happens to a fictional character in a movie.

An effective politician or leader knows how to compel his audience and get them really excited about the future—or angry about the present. These overpowering emotional extremes become the basis for initiating new action, for better or for worse. When you understand this, you learn to accept the responsibility of having so much influence over the motivations of others. An ethical business person does not abuse this power by seeking to coerce others into feeling or doing things they do not actually desire. He only helps them to understand their choices more clearly and gives them the courage to make informed decisions.

ENTREPRENEURS TALK 'AT' INSTEAD OF 'WITH' THEIR AUDIENCE

The best sales pitch in the world is a conversation. Most people, if allowed to talk for long enough, will tell you everything you need to know to get them to do what you want. This is because people love talking about two things:

1. What makes them happy.
2. What makes them unhappy.

They don't usually come out very directly and admit that, but you can pick it up through context clues if you are a careful listener. Whether they are talking about their life story, or what they do on the weekends, or what interests them, it will always be an admission of what holds emotional dominion over them. Then you can talk in a way that will show them how what you are offering works so as to move them away from what they don't like and towards what they do like. This is the backbone of your value proposition.

Most people fail at this because they come right out of the gate swinging, desperate to stuff as many generic value propositions as they can in the ears of their audience, in the hopes that one or two of them will make it past their defences and that they will buy something. This is exactly what the unfortunate *Shark Tank* entrepreneur in the last chapter did, and she paid the price when it counted most.

What she should have done was frame the conversation by introducing what it was she was going to be talking about, why the audience of investors would be interested in it, and (most importantly) what she expected them to do with such valuable information. With that context established from the very beginning, she could have easily transitioned her pitch into a two-way conversation with the focus on her audience.

In its most blunt form, it goes something like this:

> *'This is what we're talking about. This is the kind of work I do. This is what people find valuable about it, and why it's important, and why I'm bothering to tell you all this. Now tell me about you. What do you find valuable? What do you find important to you? How could you see something like this fitting into your life?'*

The reason most people cannot pull off something as simple as this is because they are not flexible. They memorize a way of talking or being and repeat it on autopilot. They spend all their energy on chasing prey down one meal at a time instead of naturally attracting what they desire. Train yourself TO REALLY LISTEN WHEN PEOPLE TALK, EVEN IN CASUAL CONVERSATION. Look for the clues they reveal about what they want.

When the time comes for you to be giving out information instead of receiving it, understand that your audience will only listen as far as they know the reason for doing so. The key to creating engagement is to tie the information being presented onto something the listener already cares about. You should read this book because it will help you to clarify what your business stands for and communicate far more effectively for greater market penetration and profit.

By introducing the book with that premise, everyone who reads it stands prepared to gain more out of it because they are interpreting the information it contains differently. They will categorize it differently within their minds from the very first chapter onward. The alternative is potentially sacrificing retention of the first sections of the book as the reader struggles to find the underlying pattern to the information and relevance to their own life. We will go more deeply into selling yourself in Section III, but for now, we turn to the process of identity introspection.

SECTION II

CREATING YOUR BRAND IDENTITY

Introduction to Creating Your Brand Identity

We don't always know what makes our own ideas valuable. Failed entrepreneurs are often very close to where they need to be to get the results they want. They just can't see the bigger picture of how everything in their brand identity could fit together as one cohesive story. However, by being asked the right strategic questions, and forced to come up with meaningful answers, rapid progress can be made.

Professional consultants will often act as though they are a member of their client's target market approaching their brand for the very first time with a specific problem. They use this setup to monitor how the entrepreneur would normally present their business to someone specifically setting themselves up to be sold. The logic is that if they can't get the message across under these tightly controlled and perfectly arranged settings, it is highly unlikely they will be able to go out in the real world where countless unpredictable variables are at play.

What happens, more often than not, is that founders come across as very boring when talking about their own creations. This is caused primarily by the fallacy already pointed out earlier—being too close to your own business. In being so close, you forget what things look like to an outsider, and you can't present your business in a way that will appeal to whatever they are specifically looking for. Nor can you identify the emotional personality elements which attract your specific group of consumers to want to work with someone like you.

The identity auditing process usually requires several rounds of going back and forth in a confrontational, yet supportive kind of way. This requires a very delicate balance between hardness and softness. The goal is to push founders just far enough outside of their comfort zone that they are forced to think in new ways about old habits. At the same time, if they are pushed too far or confronted too aggressively, they will be overwhelmed and miss the point of the process. As a result, they may lose their grasp on whatever progress they'd made up until that point in refining their vision.

The goal is to move beyond functional descriptions of what businesses do and instead focus on the profound change they create in the lives of buyers. If it is possible to respond to the way that someone describes their business with a statement like, 'So what? Is that important? Why does that matter?' their work is not yet complete. This process is only over when the stock answers are all used up and they are forced to think critically about the next words to come out of their mouth. Only then do real, meaningful answers from the deeper parts of the mind start to spring forth.

Through this process, founders are made to remove anything that does not immediately increase the perception of the value they have to deliver. They simplify and refine to make the uniqueness of their value more obvious so that their presentation of what they do successfully converts the customer's emotions to pleasant ones that grab attention and make them want to buy. That's when their confused understanding of their brand changes and they gain insight.

Once they've drilled down to these core elements of what makes their business work, it then becomes about rephrasing and re-engineering everything that they've said more attractively. The goal is to cut away all the clutter they've been distracting themselves with and just get straight down to the parts that actually deliver value and reveal emotional character traits. What makes an identity and its accompanying story work is a lot more than just having a functioning product.

KEEPING ABREAST OF UNSEEN OPPORTUNITIES IN THE MARKET

An overweight woman from Atlanta, Georgia, was able to inadvertently turn what other people saw as a disadvantage in the massage therapy industry into a powerful Unique Selling Proposition, which reportedly earns her up to $1,300 per day. Although she was once ashamed of her body, today she is the proud owner of what might be among the largest breasts in the world— size 48NN and weighing almost 16 pounds apiece.

When she finished massage school, she could not find employment anywhere in town because every existing provider was worried that she would not be able to deliver what their existing client base was looking for, or even stay on her feet all day. Her image and personality were not congruent with what the existing brand identities in the massage space were doing.

She could have stopped there and accepted that there was no market demand for her to operate as a masseuse. Instead, she started posting her own ads independently, this time capitalizing on the assets which other professionals had considered a liability. By offering specialty 'breast massages' where she would smother eager men in her uniquely oversized bosom, she was able to charge much more than the industry standard generic massage therapists.

Additionally, because few women have breasts as large as she does, and fewer of them live in her local area, and even fewer of those wishing to enter the massage industry, she is virtually immune to copycats in the marketplace coming along and trying to replicate her value proposition. As long as men desire to be covered in large breasts, she will have complete job security.

The moral of this story is to think outside the box long enough to realize that just because something is not in demand by the standard channels of exchange that already exist, does not mean there is no potential for you to create a new specialized approach and have total monopolistic control over it. If you look hard enough, you'll see similar opportunities for unconventional specialization in every modern industry niche. You don't have to reinvent the wheel; just tweak it a bit and make it your own.

GETTING TO KNOW YOURSELF

We talked about why so many useful ideas never take off in **Chapter 2: When Good Ideas Fail**. Your brand needs to fulfil a certain set of criteria for it to be memorable and attractive in the minds of consumers. Those criteria will vary depending on the audience and their predisposition, but at the very least you need ways for them to envision using your products for meaningful change in their lives, and a set of accompanying emotional values attached to their use. They need to feel these same values whenever they think of your brand, when they think of using your products, or when they picture what their life will be like afterward.

The way a brand presents itself needs a purpose. I often tell new clientele strategic details about the more interesting parts of my personal life to help start the relationship off with a shared sense of identity. The right personal anecdotes can make me stand out in their mind, as well as make them want to know more about me and my values. There's a reason I don't go into a long-winded diatribe about the details of my childhood, favourite colour, or other irrelevant trivia. It does nothing to prepare my audience's perception of who I am and how I can help them.

In this section of the book, we are going to focus on the steps that you need to take to understand your own brand identity on an internal level, before we ever worry about crafting the perfect sales pitch or colour scheme for your website.

This means, among other things:

- The specific problems your business exists to solve
- How they are packaged together into physical things and actions called products and services
- Both the experience of using your products and the end result of them
- The personality of your company and the emotions you want your clients to associate with it
- How your own enhanced perceptions of your company will change your actions and those of your entire team

These are the elements which come together to form your sense of identity as a solo professional or larger company. They define your place in the world, and they are living things that change with circumstance. Just like your identity as an individual, they respond to the new experiences you have with every passing day. They are not set-in-stone facts or points of data—but more like principles of change which ultimately determine how you respond to reality and the meaningful interactions you have in the world.

When you've taken the time to search within yourself and study the responses of the marketplace, you will have a solid foundation upon which to grow your brand. Let's get started.

5

Uncovering Your Core Values

No discussion of identity could work without first establishing your core values and how they affect your experiences in the world. Your core values are what define you on a deeper level than anything else you might consider to be part of who you are. What are they? They are the most basic beliefs which influence your behaviour. They are recurring patterns in your mind that pop up over and over to help you interpret your experiences and regulate your emotional responses.

Where they come from is more or less irrelevant, but my personal belief is that they are as bred into us since birth as our own DNA, and then activated in varying ways by the experiences we have while we are alive. The earlier the experience takes place in our lives, the stronger the effect it tends to have on our recurring worldview.

This is not to say that core values are completely fixed—only that there is a strong precedent for thinking and acting in a particular way. The longer a pattern has been established and the less open its owner, the harder it will be to alter. For better or for worse, our instructions for living all derive from these core conceptions of what will bring us the greatest possible happiness or unhappiness. We spend our entire lives attempting to move away from the negative side of this subjective spectrum and closer to the positive.

As our businesses are ultimately extensions of our identities, core values come into play there as well. Your company exists as a leveraged actor in the world—an instigator of specific types of change. The changes it creates will depend on what the people behind it interpret as good or bad, or in other words what they want to create more or less of. Even in businesses where the primary motivation is simply to make money, the ability to do so ethically depends on aligning the company's actions with the core values (conceptions of happiness and unhappiness) of a specific demographic of the people they serve.

When you understand a person's core values well enough, you can reasonably predict his or her actions under any given circumstances. That's important when trying to determine what your audience will or won't spend their money on, or how they will respond to a specific marketing campaign. It's important to understand the values that your company will come to represent in every action it takes in the world. A business is human potential scaled through technology and influence, so every choice that is made is exponentially more important.

GETTING TO THE CORE OF YOUR VALUES

There are three questions I find very valuable for getting to the core of the values held by a business. There's an endless diversity of responses that come from these simple requests, and the data gleaned by listening to the responses is highly valuable in crafting a better brand identity.

The three questions are:

1. Who are you?
2. What do you do?
3. Why should I care?

The way that someone answers the question, 'Who are you?' tells you an enormous amount of information about them, and not in the way they think it does. It can reveal their entire universe if you know how to listen. It's not so much about what they're saying as it is about how they make decisions about how to define themselves.

Whenever I ask someone this question, I'm looking for what they consider to be important and what distinguishes them from other people. I'm trying to pinpoint the script they carry around with them that makes up their self-referential sense of identity in the context of their business. We are all composed of millions of bits of information in the form of memories, abilities, preferences and tendencies that affect how we show up in the world. In that moment, when I ask a person to define themselves, they will self-select only the most important elements as they perceive them.

Your identity is nothing more than a series of thoughts you carry around in your head, some which are more important than others. We forget many of these thoughts all the time, add new ones, and keep bringing other thoughts back to life over and over again. When you ask someone who they are, they're essentially just regurgitating the thoughts they consider important to the story that's currently composing their conception of self. And that's what I'm doing when I interrogate them in this manner—I'm picking apart what they consider to be important about themselves.

Out of all the infinite possible ways that they could put words together to answer that question, they might tell me about an important part of their childhood which still affects their thoughts and actions in the present. If somebody knows how to dance salsa, but they don't immediately mention it, it's probably because they don't consider it an important part of what distinguishes them from everyone else. If it's the first thing out of their mouths, it's important to how they see themselves as an individual.

If you really listen when people talk about themselves, you'll see they tend to talk in terms of subjective pain and pleasure—although they'll very rarely actually phrase it that way. They'll speak of past events that defined them in some way, such as: 'Well, I grew up in this city…' That's history. Then they'll talk about active principles and active patterns of change that are currently relevant in their life.

When they're describing what they do, they're talking about the vehicle through which value is delivered. What does this exchange look like? How does your vehicle combust gasoline to create forward momentum? Talk about the alchemy that goes into your ability to turn base metals into gold for the people who hire you. The next step is to take that ordinary factual information and spin it into a compelling narrative that actually gets people to listen.

Narrative is the answer to the eternal question, 'Why should I care?' Most people have never had to seriously answer that question in a way that matters. It's considered rude to question why someone should care about something else that someone has shared. We are trained to automatically respect and give attention to other people when they talk. This is lethal thinking in the world of sales.

No one ever owes you an ounce of attention, least of all a stranger you are trying to convince to do something potentially injurious to themselves by giving you their time and money. The entitlement mentality we adopt in youth must be done away with if we are to succeed as entrepreneurial adults who earn the attention and respect of others with our identities.

'Why should I care?' is such a powerful question because it's not one that people are used to hearing, and they don't have a prepared response to it. That's when they actually start to think about things, and they don't just regurgitate the same old information on autopilot. It's a bit rude, and that's what catches them off guard. You may get several, 'Did you really just ask me that?' looks if you try this.

At first, most entrepreneurs will give terrible answers to this question because they are flustered and stumbling for an appropriate response that doesn't make them sound weak. People's first instinct is to defend their own ego and their appearance to the world. The unwillingness to look bad for even a moment is a major detriment to improvement. If they had a good answer to this question, odds are they wouldn't need help in the first place. Why should your prospects take the action you want them to take?

If you are honest enough with yourself to get to the heart of what motivates your actions, you will also find that it becomes a lot easier to sort out, among all the infinite business ideas you can pursue, which ones to follow. Genuine passion is what pushes entrepreneurs through periods of difficulty and uncertainty in the growth of their business. It is also what will make success the most emotionally rewarding beyond just the accumulation of capital. Knowing that you are making a very specific type of difference in the world is the most powerful incentive that exists for some people.

The answers you arrive at here will form the foundation of your brand identity and messaging strategy. When you understand yourself, you can hone your presentation in a way that generates action from others. You will appeal more strongly to others who share your ideals and reasons for doing what you do, regardless of the actual products and services you produce.

INTERNALLY IMPLEMENTING CORE VALUES

You may wonder what to do next as you come to a conclusion about what your core values consist of. Once you have discovered the cornerstone of what drives your company, it is essential not to let your core values simply exist only on paper. The key to implementing your core values is to be active with them—to turn ideas into ways of being.

As the founder of your company, it is important to lead by example. Cultivate these values from the top-down, encouraging every single employee to embrace and display the values which define your brand, all the way from the person who signs the checks to the one who turns the lights off at night. If your core values are unique and rooted in passion, your staff members will remember them. If they are memorable, they will be easy to follow. And from there, customers will start to recognize the company's commitment to their ideals.

You must see your values as a way to make your company stand out amongst others in character. Every good company will want to promise honesty, loyalty and quality. How will your company ensure a positive experience? How will your company outshine others, which offer similar products or services? It is no secret that some of the most successful businesses are glued together by core values, introduced by executives, and thoroughly implanted throughout the agency. No two companies will have the exact same values, as they will be formed by the individuals who create the company.

If you manage a team of employees, it is your duty to make sure they are all on board with the values which define your brand from day one. Do not let your core values be something that is simply recited during the initial training process. Instead, let them be a part of every workplace operation.

Your values should be seen as an opportunity to unite co-workers with the bond of a common goal. Show examples of how your employees can abide by these values during a typical workday. By demonstrating that they are not just protocol, but a lifestyle to embody, you are creating a more amicable workplace and strengthening your brand.

If one of your core values is 'community involvement,' you cannot simply state that you are involved. Be an active leader and seek ways to get involved. While living out a core value, you are also positively promoting the company. You will then become a company that makes a commitment and remains loyal to it. I have personally seen the benefits of an engaging leader who remains dedicated to the foundations of the business. What truly sets successful businesses apart is the progression of values from the three questions asked above to the formation of an enterprise.

There is no faster way to garner the lasting respect of employees, partners and consumers than to become the embodiment of an ideal. It is up to you to choose what matters to you most and what you can comfortably dedicate your life and actions to. Know yourself first and the rest will fall into place, naturally.

There is a longer series of questions I ask to help budding entrepreneurs go deeper and get to the core of their values. Several of them are listed in **Appendix 2** of this book, and more can be downloaded from www.brandidentitybreakthrough.com/free

6

Developing a Unique Selling Proposition

Uniqueness is vital to a business identity, more so today than at any other time in history. There is now more competition in the marketplace on both global and local levels than ever before. Because people make choices based on what they perceive their options to be, and they have more options with each passing day, it becomes harder to stand out as the right choice in nearly any industry.

The only time that this does not apply is when you are truly the first in a new industry, and no one else offers what you do. The very first manufacturers of flying cars may have a temporary monopoly on the market when they break ground but rest assured that imitators will soon be hot on their tail. They will need to learn to stand out or be quickly overtaken.

A by-product of this increase in marketplace variation is an increase in consumer demand. Whenever people are given the luxury of choice, they become refined in their wants. Specificity in life is a symptom of affluence, and over time, our emotional responses become attuned to a narrower range of experience. There's a reason why the wealthier people get, the pickier they become over the products they buy or how they spend their time. The more specific their desire, the more specific the solution they will seek.

Colloquially, we call this snobbery, and we are all subject to it on some level. Think of something in your life you have a highly refined taste for. For a lot of people (myself included) it's coffee or another specific food or drink. Although at this point I am undoubtedly chemically dependent upon caffeine to function normally, I refuse to drink instant coffee except in true emergency situations.

In my travels, I've had the opportunity to sample many exotic varieties of coffee beans with different growing, roasting and brewing properties. I've paid up to $20 for a single cup of Kopi Luwak in Indonesia, which is made from a coffee bean that has been eaten and excreted by a weasel-like animal that lives in the trees before being brewed. I've had life-changing coffee, terrible coffee, and just oddly interesting variations on coffee. For whatever reason, my senses are attuned to notice the very subtle differences in all of them. This allows me to make an informed buying choice among all the thousands of differentiators within the coffee industry.

Someone who doesn't even like coffee though may think they all taste only marginally different, and he or she could never fathom whatever justifies the price range from 25¢ to $20. Or if you are an audiophile like me, you've probably felt the frustration that comes when your $400 earphones don't display the minor shuffling noises of the orchestra members in their chairs on stage quite as clearly as your $600 earphones.

Outside of a few limited domains where I have expert

knowledge and give attention to detail, there is a whole world of products I will never appreciate the full detail of. I view cars as a way to get from point A to point B faster than walking. Although I use a computer every single day of my life and depend on it to maintain both my income and my social life, I only know as much about it as I must in order to have purchased a moderately nice machine I can use easily. There are worlds of detail in the market I will never fully appreciate, and they only increase as time passes.

This heightened attention to specific types of demand means there is great opportunity for any entrepreneur brave enough to come along and fill it. As a marketplace develops, producers become known for addressing the needs of the consumer in one very specific way better than anyone else in their industry. This is their Unique Selling Proposition (USP). If you want the world to take your brand seriously, you need to understand your own USP inside and out and be prepared to make it the focal point of your messaging.

HOW UNIQUENESS HAPPENS

Whenever we need a problem solved, we unconsciously assess our available options. Whether it be deciding where to go for dinner or what model a new car will be, we compare and contrast in our head the costs and benefits of everything that exists within a certain mental category. To stand out, whatever your company produces must solve a problem better than whatever already exists within the same category your audience uses when making these choices.

There was a simpler time when being unique in your sector of the market could be as easy as finding one or two differentiating factors and building a messaging strategy around them. Domino's Pizza made a name for themselves by attaching their brand to a simple, yet appealing gimmick: 30 minute delivery or your pizza is free. It was, for a time, their USP. It was just one of the many different ways they could have stood out in the market.

What if, instead of focusing on the speed of delivery, they had made superior ingredients their USP? That's the approach Papa John's pizza has taken with their iconic tagline, 'Better ingredients, better pizza, Papa John's.' Automatically, the choice between these two competitors becomes clear in the mind of the pizza buyer. If you value speed more than you value quality, purchase from Domino's. If you value quality more than you value speed, purchase from Papa John's.

The larger category of 'pizza' has now successfully been split into two distinct sub-categories: 'fast pizza' and 'quality pizza,' and this process can continue to much finer levels of distinction from there if the market supports it. While for the casual pizza eater, the two may still be more or less interchangeable, there has developed over time enough of a fan following for both of these brands that for a specific sector of the market only their favourite will do.

They're not in the mood for pizza. They're in the mood specifically for Domino's or Papa John's, and nothing else will suffice. This is the ultimate goal of having a USP—to become a market category unto yourself through the strength of what your brand represents.

Your uniqueness doesn't have to be a single specific feature that stands out about your product. In fact, making your USP a simple quality, such as being faster, bigger, lighter, shinier, or cheaper than the rest, makes it easy for your competitors to replicate your actions. If you attempt to win over the market on one factor alone, you may find yourself fighting competitors with the same idea. A more complex and secure form of uniqueness comes from a combination of many tangible and intangible factors which link practical utility with emotional values to your brand.

It could even be argued that the smaller your business, the more important it is to have a complex USP. Since you aren't reaching out to mass audiences, you don't need to worry about simplifying your message down to a single superlative for the whole world to know you as. Because you engage more intimately with a much more highly selected audience, there is room in their mind for a much more detailed analysis of the options available. Within that analysis will fall everything covered in this section of the book, including your personality (which will be covered more in the following chapter).

It is important to not only start out with a strong USP but to remain loyal and to perpetuate your USP as much as possible. Over time, it will become synonymous with your company's name or brand image, so you will need to stay committed to it. This is a long-term relationship, and the more you understand that the stronger your message will be. When you have vision over the long term, it also gives a sense of stability and security that reflects in your USP more effectively when it matters most.

YOUR DIFFERENTIATING FACTORS

If you're at a loss about where to begin, do some research into other companies in your industry and their examples of USPs. How do other companies take advantage of a unique vision? Can you even tell what is unique about them when you think of them? If you can take a look at a successful enterprise, examine their product, and find its essence, you can learn a lot about how to design your own USP.

Think of a product or advertisement that appeals to you. What is it about the message that you like? For some companies, it is the marketing not necessarily of a product, but of an idea. In many cases, car manufacturers will not just sell you a car. They also sell you the idea of what that car brings into your life. This could either be the concept of freedom, dependability, or luxury, which becomes part of their brand personality. There is the physical product itself and then what it means to the consumer. Whatever it is that helps you identify with the vehicle itself is part of their USP.

Your success depends on your ability to convince customers that you are different and better than any other options. This doesn't just mean other competitors in your industry. What you offer is a means to an end, and you need to convey that with specific, compelling information. General promises of having higher quality or better service won't cut it.

Try asking your employees. Sometimes, your Sales and Customer Service departments may know more about what your customers are buying and why they choose your company over every other option available. Otherwise, go directly to the customers themselves. You can do this by holding face-to-face conversations, surveys and focus groups.

USP consultants will often work by comparing the internal feedback they get from staff members within your organization with the external feedback that comes directly from the people who willingly spend money with your company. If a particular theme comes up consistently throughout this process, there's a good chance it may be what you should start focusing on, as the backbone of your brand identity.

Start thinking of your product both in terms of the end result gained by using it and the mechanics through which it creates that result. You may recognize these concepts more commonly referred to as benefits and features. A benefit is an effect that something has on the user. A feature is a quality of the product which creates that effect.

If you've studied any conventional sales training material, you've probably been told to disregard features and focus entirely on the benefits of your product. Generally, this is good advice. As the saying goes, 'They buy the hole, not the drill.' However, an even more powerful buying narrative is created when you combine the two causally. Your product becomes uniquely superior because it can 'do X in Y way.' An enormous amount of credibility is added to anything you say about your business when you can support it with a compelling explanation that even laymen will be able to understand.

This is the beginning of a relatively new phenomenon in marketing called Education Marketing, and we will talk about it more in **Chapter 12: How to Educate Your Audience**. It represents a major change in the way that companies present what they produce to the world. Instead of attempting to create a quick peak in positive or negative emotions, which leads to an impulsive buying decision, the producers of high-quality products can educate their buyers on useful information that sets them apart.

This is hard to do. It takes more time and dedication to your craft. It also opens up the door to a whole new universe of potential differentiating factors. If single descriptive adjectives like 'faster' or 'cheaper' are the primary colours of uniqueness, educational explanations of what your product does to produce different results are the detailed palette of hues used by a skilled painter who can expertly mix ingredients to arrive at the detail he wants.

MODE OF DISTRIBUTION

Does how you get your products to your consumers differ from others in your industry in a notable way? Domino's Pizza claimed their distribution was faster than the rest and was willing to back it up with a guarantee.

This is a lesson I know particularly well. My father was the owner of several Blockbuster Video rental stores in California for most of my life. We were financially well off throughout my upbringing, with a large house in a desirable area of North County, San Diego and more than enough amenities to keep four kids entertained every passing Christmas and birthday. So, imagine how surprised I was when my parents were forced to sell our house, and my father's Blockbuster stores were all subsequently closed.

This was in 2008, which you may recognize as the year after Netflix introduced digital streaming services to its DVD-by-mail distribution. It would take another three years for Blockbuster Video to close its remaining stores, but the die was already cast by this change. A superior method of distribution had rapidly become the new industry standard, and with every passing day, people had fewer reasons to make a physical trip to a video rental store to get their movies. The few remaining advantages that Blockbuster had over Netflix, such as the human touch and impulse items, like candy and popcorn, were not enough to sustain it.

Similarly, Amazon is rapidly dismantling longstanding

bookstores due to their superior way of getting books and other products to you. Given the option, the market has shown it would rather order these things online and wait for them in the mail than have to make the trip to a retail location. Like Netflix's video streaming service, an eBook can even be sent directly to your Kindle or other e-reader device moments after purchase. It is foreseeable that many other industries will soon follow suit, with the exception of businesses whose value proposition is based on the physical experience of being there (e.g. fancy sit-down restaurants, movie theatres, stadiums, concert halls, etc.).

Incidentally, Blockbuster refused an offer to purchase Netflix in 2000, years before they would have had to worry about a game-changing USP coming onto the scene. Keep that in mind when considering your own differentiating factors. Is what you offer so radically superior that it could completely change the way people buy in your industry?

METHOD OF CONSUMPTION

How your audience uses your products is also a major part of how you can differentiate from your competition. In the above example of Netflix versus Blockbuster, the most common method of consumption in each case was on a TV versus on a computer. Both are selling the same category of products: movies. For the purposes of this illustration, ignore for a moment that Netflix now offers its own exclusive programming and countless other titles that would never have been found in a Blockbuster Video store.

Even if you are watching the exact same movie, the method of consumption changes the experience drastically. Netflix is famous (or infamous) for enabling users to 'binge watch' hours of their favourite shows and movies. While this was also possible with VHS tapes and DVDs, it was less convenient. You'd have to plan ahead or physically get up to change one disc to another.

With Netflix's enormous digital library available at only a few clicks of a mouse, viewers often fall into a pattern of not leaving the screen all day, just going from one entertaining distraction to another. This has become one of the hallmarks of Netflix's core audience, along with other new categories of activity like the more recent introduction of 'Netflix and chill.' So far as I know, it means using Netflix bingeing as an excuse and/or opportunity to initiate low-pressure sexual activities with an interested party. What a fascinating and unpredictable world we live in.

How does the way your audience uses your product, sets you up for differentiation from everyone else? Is your electronic device designed to work underwater? Think of the many possible applications this could create for the marketplace. Do you teach knitting privately via webcam or in a large in-person group setting? What are the advantages and disadvantages of each approach, and how will they influence consumer impressions and behaviour? These are the layers of differentiation which are exposed when you start to look at your business and its products beyond the surface level of the basic problem that they solve.

INTERACTION WITH YOUR BRAND

The experience a consumer has with your brand is a type of relationship. They interact with you in countless ways—when they read the text on your website, when they are greeted at the entrance to your store by a member of your staff, or get your advertising jingle stuck in their head. This is where brand personality becomes paramount.

Many industries, such as the restaurant industry, become known not just for the quality of their food, but the quality of service or an uncommon gimmick incorporated into their atmosphere. All of these have a profound impact on the emotions your consumers experience when consuming your products and, in turn, the lingering emotions they continue to carry long afterward. These often understated qualities are actually a major part of the reason why consumers form strong relationships and loyalty—and they have nothing to do with how good the food is.

The purpose of your USP is to help customers view your product or service as the only choice for their needs. If you can strategically design your USP to incorporate many potential differentiating points into one coherent narrative, you will immediately overcome your customers' buying objections. It is possible, with enough introspection, for your USP to become a detailed story of the nuanced experience of the value you offer. That level of uniqueness can last for the lifetime of your company and adapt for generations with the ebb and flow of the market.

Once you've developed your winning USP, your goal is to start integrating it into your brand. Internally, this means adjusting your own mindset about your business and training your staff to uphold the new company culture. This culture is a living thing that replicates in the minds of your staff, no matter how large your organization.

Externally, the story of your USP will become the backbone

of all your marketing materials. The conversation you have with your customers will revolve around the unique experience of buying from you and how their lives will be better because they do. Section III will cover the topic of telling your story to the world. Keep reading to learn about the most human element of your brand: your personality profile.

7

Crafting Your Personality Profile

Your brand identity is more than the practical value of the things you produce. Whatever you choose to put out into the world is a product of your core values. It exists to solve a specific problem and make people feel a certain way as they interact with your brand. The specific way you want them to feel when they think of you is your personality profile—and there is a much larger range of possibilities here than you might assume.

We all play characters in the larger narrative of the world around us. If you don't choose for yourself what kind of character you want others to treat you as, the world will do it for you without your consent. The same is true of your company's brand. As soon as you grow big enough to be noticed, people will begin to form strong conceptions about the character of your business. They will make up in their own mind what kind of people run it and what they are really motivated by. They will choose adjectives to align your brand with, whether you like it or not. The solution is to establish a strong brand personality before anyone has the chance to impose their projections on you.

Consumers interact with brands as though they are actual people with real personalities, preferences and pastimes. Entrepreneurs with a more technical mindset can get so caught up in the tangible elements of their products; they completely lose sight of the user experience. This is why it is quite common for start-ups to have, at a minimum, one technical co-founder who is in charge of product development, and another marketing co-founder who is in charge of representing the brand to the world.

Have you neglected the personality attributes of your own brand? They are more important than you might think because the success of your business depends on more than just solving a problem well. When your customers buy their first product from you, they should be entering into a long-term relationship based on trust and the memory of positive experiences. Brand personality is about being deliberate and crafting that experience in such a way that it supports your business goals while serving your audience the solutions to their problems.

How people feel when they think about your brand is actually one of the easiest ways to differentiate yourself from your competitors. You will recall from the last chapter that USP development is crucial to your success. Personality probably doesn't require you to redesign your products and change manufacturing specifications. It won't necessarily mean you need to re-staff or train new types of specialists within your organization. It just means you have to start thinking about your company differently—and to make sure those thoughts are properly carried out to everyone else.

BRAND PERSONALITY OF A TEENAGE STREET MUSICIAN

One of my very first entrepreneurial outings took place when I was sixteen years old. By accident, a musical friend and I discovered we could make money by sitting on the public sidewalk, just outside a 7-11 on the coast highway in North County, San Diego with our instruments and playing for tips. Between us, we had an acoustic guitar and a violin, and we knew a few simple arrangements of popular classic rock songs that the tourists who visited San Diego for the beach every summer seemed to really enjoy. I think we made $40 between us the first time we went out to play on a Saturday afternoon. That was all the validation we needed to go back out there every weekend and play again.

Over time, we optimized our approach because we paid close attention to what prompted people to leave tips more often and in higher amounts. We pooled the money we were making to reinvest it into our fledgling operation in the form of a battery powered 50-watt amplifier, microphones and cables so that we could extend our reach and attract a larger audience. We cleaned up our appearance so that we would come across more as ambitious overachievers than as desperate beggars. We wanted people to feel good about giving us a dollar or twenty as they passed by and were impressed by what they heard.

It didn't take long for us to notice there were reliable patterns in the behaviour of our ever-changing audience of pedestrian listeners. Certain blocks of time produced far more money than others, as did certain days of the week, and times of the year. Street fairs and other outdoor events were always a major cash grab for us. People would often stop in the middle of their day's activities to form a small crowd in front of us and listen for several tunes in a row before thanking us and leaving a tip.

I don't think I'll ever forget the first time a complete stranger dropped a $100 bill in my guitar case as he walked by. We immediately stopped playing to ask him if he realized he had just given us so much money. He responded with a weary smile saying that he had been going through a really rough time and seeing the two of us out there, being so young but having so much talent and good taste in music, was the best thing that had happened to him all week. Wheels began turning in my head, which have continued spinning more than ten years later because of innocent conversations like that.

We were initially concerned about the noise disturbance we were potentially creating for local businesses on the busy avenue where we camped out and jammed. On the contrary, we soon found ourselves invited by the owners of cafes and shops to play right out in front, because our performances served to bring in more business and entertain their customers. This was my first exposure to the idea of mutually beneficial business partnerships, and we were eventually asked to play at parties and even a wedding.

Audience feedback helped us to adapt to the demands of our market. We learned that they liked seeing a duo so young who had clearly put a lot of work into learning our craft and coming up with innovative renditions of classic songs, which appealed to the nostalgia of our more mature fans. I would arrange the chordal structure of whatever we were playing into a detailed voicing and driving strum pattern, while my partner improvised on the original melody of the song with unconventional rock fiddle stylings. We had a signature sound unlike anything our audience had ever heard before, and it was because we were able to take something old and proven but change it just enough to make it new.

That unique combination of old musical tastes, creative modern stylings, and our youthful endearing personalities brought us to where we could count on making $200 to $300 per hour on a busy day—not bad for being two self-employed high school students practicing their passion on weekends. Unsurprisingly, though, this scheme ceased to be nearly as effective the moment we got old enough to grow facial hair and look like real adults begging for money.

The only thing that changed was the perceived personality and the accompanying emotions behind our 'brand.' It's cute when it's teenagers panhandling for your hard-earned cash. When its adults, you just wonder why they haven't gone out and gotten real jobs like the productive members of society they ought to be by now. Our product didn't actually change. We still played the same songs with the same level of proficiency. But factors beyond our control changed the cultural perception of our narrative. Our personality profiles had evolved into something new, and we had to change our entire business model as a result.

To this day, whenever I see musicians playing for money on street corners, I still mentally dissect what they are doing well and how they could change their performance and personality to make more money for the same effort based on my own years of experimentation in the field.

EVERYONE IS A MINOR NARCISSIST

People respond to specific personalities because they see things that they identify within themselves or desire to identify with.

Remember, everyone is an egomaniac to some degree. We all love ourselves and hold our own existence in high esteem by default. It's a built-in survival mechanism. Our brain's job is to take care of ourselves first and foremost, or else everything else we do becomes impossible. Because we love ourselves so very much, we all want to be associated with brands that we respect or provide us with an opportunity to gain respect from others.

On the other hand, the personalities we hate are those that run counter to our own values or internal narrative. There's a powerful campaign against the biotech company Monsanto among consumers of organic food because in their opinion the actions and intentions embodied by Monsanto are against their best interests. They have chosen to value producing food without the use of synthetic pesticides or genetic modification. Likewise, the supporters of these types of biotechnology often hold the organic industries in contempt for turning public opinion against their own values.

The point is that people don't make buying decisions based on a product's practical utility alone. They do things that affirm their own sense of identity because ultimately nothing leads to a greater sense of lasting happiness. Problems are solved in an instant. Your sense of identity is carried with you in every waking moment. Those who share common ground in their respective identities will congregate together in churches, clubs, communities, and intentional societies for the same reason. This is why social connectors are more valuable now than they have ever been before.

There's a reason why our ears naturally perk up and our attention kicks in when we think we hear our own name mentioned in a conversation. We want to know more about anything that has to do with ourselves. Your brand personality and communication style must be designed to grab the attention of your audience in the same way they are compelled to listen when they think something is about them. In **Chapter 9: How to Sell Who You Are**, we will talk about the finer details of communicating in a way which makes your target audience feel like you are talking specifically to them and appealing directly to their interests.

THE DANGER OF NARRATIVE INCONGRUENCE

Once you have decided upon a personality for your business to embody, you must remain consistent with it. Everything from the way you speak and write, to the things you claim to care about all, work to form a mental impression in the mind of your audience. When they have become accustomed to thinking of you in one particular way, it is mentally jarring to witness your brand behaving in another way.

This is narrative incongruence. It's the same as when you watch a character in a book, movie, or TV show act in a way that is considered 'out of character.' They fail to conform to the rules that have been established for them within the context of that universe. It is the quickest way to break viewer immersion and turn whatever level of engagement they had in the story against you. In real life, it can turn loyal fans into vocal haters who feel betrayed by your sudden change in appearance. Remember: your biggest fans are the ones who identify most strongly with you. To betray their expectations is an attack upon their sense of identity.

Be cautious about taking an approach to your brand personality which is exclusively calculated to get a specific kind of response from your audience. It has to be something that comes naturally to you and the people behind the scenes of your company. Otherwise, every action you take will run the risk of betraying the illusion of who you really are. When that happens, you will have lost whatever goodwill you had cultivated in the minds of your audience.

McDonald's, for example, has been working to reverse the public's unhealthy perception of their food. They have introduced healthy menu items to try to appeal to mainstream concerns specifically. While healthier food may be an admirable ambition, it isn't necessarily the smartest branding move for them. It isn't congruent with the previous elements of their brand that brought them to global marketplace dominance. The public can sense the dissonance and inauthenticity in their choice of offering healthy menu items, and it makes little positive impression on the type of people who already identify with them as their fans.

Build a character around your business and stay consistent with it. Apply what you have learned about yourself, your business, and your audience to create messages about your products. Use that character to engage in real relationships with your clients on the common ground of values you both mutually embody (or at a minimum, respect).

THE EMOTIONAL ELEMENTS BEHIND YOUR BRAND

Why did you get into the business you are in? Hopefully, the reasons run deeper than merely having spotted an opportunity for profit in the marketplace.

I went into education very early in my professional development due to my natural capacity for it, and to develop my skills through real-world implementation. Most importantly,

I cared deeply about helping others to increase their own working knowledge. It remains one of my core values. The fact that there was enough market demand for me to make a living through teaching and mentorship was just a happy coincidence which enabled me to survive while I pursued my passion.

To be successful as the kind of educator I aspired to be, I had to be a person others wanted to bring into the lives of their children. It was about both the process of learning and the end result of new knowledge. The emotional requirements of my profession inspired me to become supportive, direct, challenging, inquiring, and encouraging in the eyes of my students. Because education is such a genuine passion of mine, it was not necessary to fake any aspects of my personality in order to present myself as the appropriate kind of brand personality for the circumstances.

My uniqueness as an educator came primarily in my method of interaction. While there were plenty of ways to learn the things I taught, it would have been extremely difficult to find anyone else who could emulate the exact same relationship dynamics that I cultivated with my clients. The unique combination of skills, experience and demeanour combined into a strong personality, which was possible because I knew my strengths so well. It applies just as much (if not more) in the case of larger organizations who have little personal interaction with their audience.

If you run a large company which produces products or services for travel, what emotional qualities naturally match what your intended audience will find appealing? To answer that, all you have to do is understand why people travel. They travel for freedom. They travel for self-expression. They travel to push boundaries. They travel to learn about the world. They travel for adventure. Business travellers have their own entirely different reasons for packing their things up and getting on a plane to new places, so these personality traits can be further and further refined by sub-genre.

Your goal with personality branding will be to get your audience to feel these things before they actually complete a purchase with you. They should automatically associate these feelings with your logo, your marketing copy, or anything else that you produce. You can artificially induce that specific emotional win-state by creating a sensation of familiarity and intuitive confidence that whatever you are offering will lead your buyers toward the goal they seek. When you can combine this with a product offering that produces a specific, demonstrable result, you will have the foundation of a brand that will accomplish amazing things.

If you have a business, it's safe to assume that you have already spent some time thinking about congruence in your brand identity. You may have even spent hours trying to figure out how you can find alignment between yourself, your business, your audience and your products. It can be quite difficult to get this right, but when you do, you will realize how crucial it is to the success of your business.

YOU DON'T HAVE TO BE THE FACE OF YOUR COMPANY

Many founders are understandably shy about becoming a mascot for their own business. That's okay. Just because a business needs a personality does not mean it must be your own personality or even that of any person in particular. Remember, a brand ultimately becomes a character unto itself, with bits and pieces taken from strategic sources and presented interactively to the world. A brand does not need to encompass every trait of its creator to be authentic.

Branding a company with your own personality works best when the value proposition is directly tied to the experience of working with you. If your value proposition is brake pads with a longer lifespan, it will make sense to build your brand personality around things like safety, security and trust. Whoever the founder is will have little to do with the buying decisions of that particular industry, unless he or she is someone who is already known for those qualities.

To get the best of both worlds, many companies hire professional personalities to endorse them, especially in industries that are home to heroes with existing fan bases. If Michael Jordan endorses Nike, Nike benefits from the association as he has spent his entire athletic career building as someone driven, motivated, focused and friendly. Nike doesn't have to build that all for themselves from the ground up because Jordan has already done it as a by-product of his fame in athletics. Those are the values their buyers like to see within themselves, and the motivation they have for making the purchase.

Few of the people who admire professional athletes and their brand personalities will ever come close to accomplishing the same physical achievements. By being a fan, they get to experience a few of the same emotional thrills by proxy without ever having to step onto the field or dedicate their life to mastery of the skill. None of the people who read a Superman comic book will ever leap tall buildings in a single bound, but the personality brand of Superman is undoubtedly one of the strongest in the world and continues to inspire smaller acts of heroism with the virtues he stands for across countless media.

If you understand your audience and product well enough,

try to picture the character they would most want to purchase from. In this sense, your brand personality is the bridge between buyer and product. The better you understand those two sides of the equation, the easier it will be to see the best way to connect the personality junction.

Taking the time to consider and understand your audience thoughtfully will then inform every business decision you make. With a clear vision of who you are interacting with and exactly what they need, you will know what products to offer and what message to send out.

Building a bridge between your buyer and your product is a matter of being willing to explore certain elements more deeply. It is important to consider these questions carefully and take the time to reflect on them.

- What is the intrinsic value of your products? What practical problem do they solve?
- What is the emotional value of your products? How do they make people feel? What values do they represent?
- What is unique or uncommon about your business compared to others in the same industry?
- Where did the inspiration for the business come from? How did you end up here of all places? What obstacles did you have to overcome along the way?
- Is your own personality/image a major part of the appeal of your business? Do you want it to be?
- What valuable information can you provide about what your business stands for, beyond your actual products?

Creating a clear, strong foundation for your brand will provide the support, structure, and guidance that are needed to make smart business decisions, both internally and externally.

8

Knowing Your Target Audience

A popular sales proverb states that the most important ingredient of success in business is having a hungry audience. Your target audience is the group of people who care about what your product does because it has a direct, favourable effect on their lives. They are the ones who will genuinely be bettered by the inclusion of your narrative within their lives, not the people who you will have to trick or coerce to become your customers.

One of the first things I ask anyone starting a new business is, 'Who or what is your perfect customer or client?' No one business can compete with everyone, so having a focus is a top priority. Anything which exists to service everyone really exists to service no one. Finding a specific niche will keep you focused and competitive, and allow your business to soar very highly within that niche.

If you understand your own USP and personality profile, it is not very difficult to paint a very specific picture of the kind of person who is going to be attracted to working with you. Conversely, if you already know your target audience, it is much easier to design a product and brand personality around it. Knowing any one of these specific elements about your business makes it significantly easier to figure out the others. The right answers for your business will gradually come into focus the more you introspect and study the conditions of the market.

The best quality product or the most innovative marketing tactic won't matter if the people you are approaching don't see a need for what you offer. The most expensive yacht in the world will be worthless to someone who hates water. Gourmet coffee is of no use to someone who doesn't drink it. A fish simply doesn't need a bicycle. An enormous part of winning the game of market success is knowing precisely, who you are working to serve and to whom you will be speaking when you promote yourself.

To figure out who your hungry audience is, you need to intimately understand what it is that makes your products uniquely appealing from an outsider's perspective, as well as the way your sector of the market makes important buying decisions. This is why, all things being equal, it is good for entrepreneurs to go into businesses they already have a lot of exposure to. When in doubt, start with what you know.

Companies can put years into building and promoting themselves on the wrong selling points because no one ever stopped to ask the market itself what they appreciated most. As we've touched upon already, being too close to your own product makes you biased about it and blind to hidden marketing opportunities.

CONSTRUCTING YOUR IDEAL CLIENT PROFILE

Constructing an ideal client profile consists of identifying all the different compelling aspects of your brand, and then comparing them to what you know about the people who make purchases in your industry.

Unless you take these steps to understand who your perfect client is, you will always waste a huge amount of your efforts. Your entire product design and communication style will be misdirected. You will struggle helplessly from one conversion to the next, just waiting for the rare opportunity actually to engage someone's interest. Targeting the wrong client turns an easy task into a stressful nightmare.

So, how do you find that specific niche to target? Start by looking at current or prospective customers and think about all the reasons why they would choose to buy from you. Make a list of your products or services, and next to each one, write down all the benefits that each one provides. Think about the types of people that would benefit from each element of your business. Take into consideration factors such as age, gender, location, the levels of education and income, occupation, or any other demographic factor you feel is relevant to how they buy.

Successful businesses in the fitness industry, for example, look at a particular age group gender, and location. They might market to middle-aged women who are struggling with their weight and also their sense of self-worth as they age. They add to this other factors such as women who have a household income within a small range, maybe $75,000 to $100,000 a year. Furthermore, these women must live within 30 minutes' drive of the fitness centre in order to be viable as potential clients.

This might bring the list of potential clients down

dramatically, but marketing to their specific needs will ensure a greater rate of return on investment on marketing dollars, because the message is uniquely targeted to customers that are listening. Marketing to a bigger market is a mistake that many small businesses make in the beginning. Unless you have a product that can be consumed by literally thousands of people a day, like bottled water, for example, you really need to focus on one particular group.

The relevant demographic factors will be very different for every industry. Depending on what you produce, it may not matter whether your clients are 20 or 60 years old. It may not make much difference if they are men or women, or how tall they are, or what their favourite television shows are.

Sometimes, a factor may be only indirectly related. For example, this book is aimed at prospective and practicing entrepreneurs. Since these types of people are more likely to be between the ages of 25 and 40 than say, 12 or 85, it makes a lot of sense for me to focus on this approximate age group. However, there is nothing in here which would necessarily exclude someone outside of that range of years.

GET TO KNOW YOUR CUSTOMER EXPERIENCE INTIMATELY

The way your customers experience purchasing and using your products might be very different than how you assume it is. Have you ever actually taken the time to approach your own business from the perspective of a completely new customer with no prior familiarity?

If you operate a business with a physical location, such as a retail store or dentist's office, what do your customers go through from the moment they pull into the parking lot to the time they leave? Is your store or office set up in a way that facilitates the decision-making process and user experience? If you primarily run your business online, what does it feel like to navigate your website?

When it comes to actually using your product or service, which elements of its functionality make it easier or more attractive for specific types of people?

In all likelihood, the product or service that you are offering is designed to save your audience time, effort, or money. If, however, the process they have to go through in order to buy or learn about your product involves wasting any of those three things, then they won't even bother.

Even if they want it badly enough to make it through the obstacles you've put in their way, their initial perception of the product is going to be a negative one, and you will already be in a disadvantaged position. The chances are that there are other people offering a similar product or service. If it is easier for your customers to get it elsewhere—even if it is an inferior product—many will choose to do that.

Never before have people been so motivated by time, and in particular, the idea of saving it. Our attention spans are shorter than ever. Anything that takes more than a couple of clicks is too much work. The burden falls on you to go to any lengths possible to eliminate any obstacles standing in the way of the customer getting access to what you sell.

WHAT ARE YOUR COMPETITORS DOING?

Another way to find your perfect audience is to take a close look at your competitors. By understanding your competition, you will gain the ability to identify their strengths and weaknesses. This will allow you to find out what they are doing so you can make your company stand out from theirs, and in turn, find out what you can offer to attract specific clients to your company.

You should seek to emulate their strengths as much as is equitable for you to with your time and money resources, but even more importantly you should look for whatever holes they aren't filling in the market. Learning more about your competition will enable you to meet customer's needs that other companies are not and allow you to see what you are up against and keep you proactive in your offerings.

Remember, it's never in your best interest to become an exact clone of someone else's success. They have a head start on you and plenty of existing loyalty in that specific sector of the market. If you understand what they are doing well, you can tweak it enough to make it something new that addresses a problem they weren't completely satisfying before you came along. You may find that some of the people who shopped with your competition only did so because it was the closest match to what they were looking for, but still left them yearning for something better.

A good example of this principle is the extremely popular dating app, Tinder. Tinder has spread far and wide around the world, in part because it is so simple to use. Tinder allows men and women to upload a limited number of pictures and a very short description of themselves in a basic profile. They are then randomly matched with members of the opposite sex in whatever location they choose and are given the opportunity to choose whether or not to initiate a conversation by swiping right or left if they like what they see. If both parties swipe right on each other, they are allowed to message each other.

Tinder has a reputation for being used primarily by young people looking to 'hook up' with each other—to have sex with little obligation. This is not surprising, considering that the only real matching criteria in their system are age, location and physical appearance. While those looking for superficial romantic flings may be the primary target audience, there are also plenty of people who use it for casual dating, serious relationships, and even just platonic friendships (or so they claim to save face). Why would they use such a simple interface for something it clearly isn't designed for?

Although there are plenty of other services specifically designed for other kinds of relationships, none of them offer the simplicity of use that Tinder does. Websites like OkCupid and Plenty of Fish generally require users to spend several hours filling out lengthily written profiles, answering personality quizzes, and browsing many similarly complicated profiles before escalating the communication from messages to phone calls, and finally meeting in person. For better or for worse, Tinder is designed to expedite that process based on as few inputs as possible. Therefore, even though Tinder is not ideal for what they want, its ease of use as a mobile app is too appealing to ignore.

What does this mean for other entrepreneurs who want to enter the online or mobile dating industry? They should learn from what Tinder does well, and adapt it for their own USP, personality and target audience. If someone could properly implement 'Tinder for serious relationships,' which replicates Tinder's simplicity with a personality and messaging strategy designed to appeal to people looking for long-term partners, they could have a powerful business.

Even though the specific market is probably much smaller,

they could have complete dominance over it. Many of the people who begrudgingly use Tinder due to lack of a superior alternative for their needs would quickly migrate over to the new platform.

THE BRIDGE BETWEEN YOUR COMPANY AND YOUR AUDIENCE

Your company profile and audience profile are two sides of the same coin. It should be your priority to build both of them in tandem as you progress. It is only when you have a clear image of these two concepts that you can start to build a bridge of communication between them. Developing your USP and personality profile are covered in chapters 6 and 7 of this book, respectively. Coming up next, Section III will focus specifically on the art and science of communication in business.

The bridge of communication acts to draw clients to your business and allows you to showcase the uniqueness of what you have to offer. It's a two-way process. Just because one company was very good at marketing hamburgers, this didn't put other companies off from doing the same. In fact, the success of many businesses offering a similar product comes down to the 'bridge' they build between their similar products and distinct company profiles.

This should be obvious, but it is one of the biggest problems entrepreneurs face when struggling with the dilemma of what to do next. You can't really create an effective marketing campaign without knowing first and foremost what kind of person should be reading it. Yet, the majority of advertising focuses foremost on product attributes, ignoring the mentality of the viewer.

Knowing your audience is crucial, but it is not the whole story. Once you have found your target audience, you then need to learn everything you can about them. The smaller and more specific this group is, the easier this will be. This is another reason to zoom in as far as possible when deciding who your market is.

The information you need to know includes obvious things, such as how they currently get the product you are offering, to subtler but equally important data. How does your target group of people prefer to take in information? Different people prefer different ways of learning new things and expanding their interests, including websites, magazines, television commercials, or just word of mouth through a trusted group of friends. What aspirations do they have? What motivates them?

The more you know about them, the better you can target your messaging. The right people will be more likely to actually see it, and also far more likely to respond to it when they do because it will appeal to something they actually care about deeply.

You should also consider that your product may very well appeal to two or more different markets. This is obviously a good thing, as the more value you provide, the better, but you need to realize that they are two separate markets. Your marketing approach may ignore one of those groups entirely, effectively eliminating half of your potential client base. By segmenting your audience into its relevant categories and niches, you can then target each one on its own individual characteristics.

Market mediums change over time. People of all demographics are becoming more sophisticated in their buying habits. Ten years ago, people over 50 would have rarely used the internet in the first place to seek out product information or go shopping. Now they are doing it on their smartphones nearly everywhere they go. You need to keep up with these changing trends, or your product will be perceived to be irrelevant. This is a crucial part of the process of entrepreneurial adaptation, and it requires you to know the habits of your buyers.

Tailoring your approach to a specific audience doesn't only apply to the medium, but also to the content itself. The choice of words, tone and approach will vary tremendously depending on the demographic you are aiming at. The age, level of education, and the gender of those you are addressing will all influence your choice, so it is absolutely crucial that you know as much as possible about those you are reaching out to.

This goes for other businesses as much as it does for consumers. If you are selling directly to organizations, you will need to know who to contact in those organizations, and at what level of technical expertise you will be dealing with. You may have the most convincing argument in the world, but if it is pitched at the wrong level, it will sail over the head of the person making the purchasing decision.

The time, effort, and money you spend on discovering who your target audience is and how to reach them will be well worth it. Without that preparation, you are in danger of not only wasting your time and money, but also of making a poor impression on the people who make your success possible.

SECTION III

TELLING YOUR STORY TO THE WORLD

Introduction to Telling Your Story to the World

Communication is happening in every shared moment, and in ways that are not always obvious. It happens in the way your hair falls on a given day. It happens in how straight you are standing or the way you walk into a room. The clothing you wear tells a significant story about who you are. There are so many other things we take for granted about the messages we send out to the world.

Many people don't want to spend money on a product or a service they can't identify with. They want to feel a connection of trust based on a sound relationship. The problem with marketing in today's rapid digital climate is that you only have a few seconds to establish this connection.

Sales is about learning to direct the information you put out towards a specific outcome—getting others to think the way you want them to think about our business. When they agree with you about the value you are offering, they will be ready to take the actions you want them to take. This can be done unethically (by tricking someone into a sale with false premises and incomplete information) or ethically (through education and emotional support).

To be an effective communicator is to be absolutely clear with your core message. If your goal is to attract members of the opposite sex romantically, there is a combination of factors which will aid you most in that mission. However, these factors may not be compatible with other goals you have, such as appearing intelligent, intimidating, easy-going, unconventional, or something else entirely. Since you can't be all things to all people all the time, you have to pick what is important to you and then stay consistent with it.

For your brand identity to be effective, it is imperative that you understand the intended outcome of all the subtle information it sends out into the world. In this section of the book, we will focus on turning the core components of your brand identity into a presentation that deserves the attention of your target audience.

Sometimes, the goal of your communications will be the completion of a new customer's very first purchase. In other contexts, it will be upselling them into something larger than what they initially bought. You will need to know how to motivate people to take immediate action with new information you have handed out.

Maybe you are at a point in your business where you are not so much focused on immediate cash-for-product sales, but more so on the longer-term goal of reputation building. In this case, your goal will be to plant seeds of trust and authority in the minds of your audience. You will be the first option they turn to when they are faced with a problem you are prepared to solve. Immediate sales and long-term branding are not always compatible, but a wise communicator can accomplish both with a comprehensive messaging strategy.

There will be times when you aren't concerned about what

your consumers think at all. Sometimes you will only need to address other professionals who have no desire to buy from you. Their interest will revolve around your potential for commerce, not as the producer of a specific type of value. They will either see you as a threat, partner, or investment opportunity.

If they view you as a threat, your goal should be to intimidate them enough so that they will not attempt to invade your market territory. If they view you as a partner, your goal should be to show them how they stand to profit by working with you. If they view you as an investment, your goal should be to demonstrate your competence and viability in the market.

Lazy entrepreneurs limit their communication with consumers to traditional impression-based marketing techniques. They rely on taglines, catchy names, and other superficial branding schemes to create vague associations with their company. Small businesses should instead be educating the world about previously unknown or unavailable opportunities for personal happiness.

By learning how to be a better communicator, you will gain access to a wide new world of opportunities which are only available if you know how to talk in a way that makes others want to listen. Knowledge and ability can only take you so far. It is our relationships with others that make it possible for our individual actions to have greater meaning—but only if you master the art of influence.

Whatever the base of what you are trying to get across, it will only be amplified when you apply the fundamentals of good communication.

UNDERSTANDING YOUR COMMUNICATION GOALS

Until you know what you want to accomplish, it's impossible to measure progress. Before you can begin crafting a communication strategy, you need to have honed your specific identity first. How are you supposed to know what combination of taglines, slogans, symbols, colour schemes and personas will create the most favourable impression in the minds of your target audience if you haven't analyzed what they are looking for? How can you display your best self if you hardly know who that is?

In the last section, we covered the types of questions you need to be asking yourself and the ways that your perspective will have to change in order to bring your core values to the forefront of your business. These values go on to shape the overall personality of your brand, and how your products, and services can be displayed uniquely to a very specific sector of the market. Since we now understand what we are trying to say, our focus turns to the best ways to say it. This is where we enter the domain of sales and marketing.

There's a reason why sales and marketing are the banes of many founders. I get it. You've worked so hard just developing your products and bringing your business together. Now, suddenly, you must convince someone else that your business is worth paying attention to? You must talk to complete strangers and get them to hand over their money simply because you said so? It's a loathsome process for people who aren't natural-born communicators.

Whether you plan to be in charge of your own sales and marketing or not, every founder should understand the fundamentals of their communication strategy. It will be integral to the way that you train your employees, bring on new partners, expand your product line, and grow your audience. If nothing else, it should leave you far better prepared to delegate these tasks to the most qualified people in the best possible way.

Let's make a very important distinction here between sales and marketing because the two are often vaguely grouped as one process. The truth is that though they are related and complementary, they remain distinct functions of any business. It is possible for a business to do one very well, and almost completely neglect the other. Likewise, you may have a strong talent for one but be totally hopeless with its counterpart. That's okay. The key to improvement is understanding where your weaknesses lie and then systematically improving them.

Sales is the process of converting non-customers into customers or increasing the purchase quality and frequency of existing customers. It is what creates direct revenue for your business, and in many ways is what makes your business 'legitimate.' Put simply, without sales, you don't have a business.

Marketing is the act of increasing awareness of your brand. Its purpose is to get more people to know who you are or remind the ones who already do why they should care about your existence. It doesn't necessarily lead to a direct increase in revenue. Many of the people who know who you are may never actually buy anything from you. It's a very powerful branding position to be in when even people who will never have any use for what you sell recognize you as a market leader in your industry or associate you with a specific desirable feature.

Even non-customers who recognize you can contribute to the network effect that passes your brand along until it reaches the mind of an ideal customer.

The reason why sales and marketing are often confused

with each other or grouped together is because one can directly lead into the other. You need people to be aware of your solution before they can be convinced to buy it. On a small enough scale, both actions can be accomplished at once, almost seamlessly. However, as you grow, it's going to make more and more sense to segregate the two, as this will increase the efficiency of both. To perform both of these tasks, you will need to hone your communication skills.

What you choose to communicate can vary, but it will most likely include some combination of the following:

- Mission and vision statements about why your company exists
- A message from the founder or CEO about past achievements, experiences and goals
- The history of the company (or what lead to its creation)
- Information about the core staff and extended personnel
- Your current and future product line
- Promotional events you are planning

Your message should be personal. It should be about the real people who have helped shape and hone your company to date. Many successful company profiles are written in the first-person perspective. They talk about the individual's dreams, hopes, and goals, both within the company and on a personal level. It is crucial to include other members of your team in order to create a holistic view of your company. Staff profiles should explain what their position is, but also how a particular person has helped to shape the company. Great company profiles also include how each staff member can assist the customer.

Whatever your goal is, the skills you acquire here will prove invaluable in both your business and personal life. Anytime you want to get something done that requires the collaboration of other people, effective communication is the catalyst which makes it possible. As you develop your ability to speak, write, and present yourself favourably, make it a point to put these tactics into practice as soon as possible. Not only will you retain the information better, but you will be emotionally encouraged to continue when you see the tangible effects of better communication.

Mastering the art of communication will make people want to work with you, and customers want to buy from you. It's the single most impactful thing you could change to improve your opportunities.

If you did nothing else well but communicate effectively, you would still go very far in business and in life.

9

How to Sell Who You Are

Positioning your product or service in the market is about getting enough people to see that the value they will receive is greater than any other way they could spend their money. It's not just other people in your industry that you are competing with. It is literally every other product on the market, and even every other activity they could be spending their time doing. Money and time remain finite for even the richest and most powerful people in the world. Whenever you spend five dollars on a cup of coffee, that cup is competing with ballet lessons for your daughter or leather seat covers for your car.

Additionally, each buying decision can be broken down into a series of smaller decisions made in mere moments. A cup of coffee is not just a cup of coffee anymore. Do I want decaf? Do I want a latte? Do I want a cappuccino? Do I want a half-decaf dark roast caramel mocha Frappuccino with whipped cream? Those all fall under different categories of choice within the initial choice to purchase coffee. Austrian economist Ludwig von Mises provided a concentrated study on the mechanics of human decision in his magnum opus, *Human Action*. He showed how the micro-actions of individual people combine to create market trends within large-scale economies.

Selling is when you transfer useful information and emotional motivation to others, in order to get them to take an action in their own best interest which they otherwise would not have taken. It is about helping others to help themselves make better decisions in their own subjective pursuit of happiness. When you sell yourself, you are helping someone to understand how you can help them improve their own life and giving them the support that they need to overcome any emotional resistance to taking action with you.

An ethical salesperson does not attempt to convince someone to do something they do not believe is in their best interest. However, if you know something would help someone else, wouldn't you do everything you could to help that person see it themselves? No matter how you currently feel about talking about yourself or your business, this is the attitude you must adopt if you want to be successful in sales. Ultimately, whether or not you personally end up handling the sales for your company, as a leader you still need to know this fundamental strategy for converting new clients and sharing your story.

The title of this chapter has been chosen very deliberately. Put the focus on selling who you are because that's the ultimate goal of branding. You are presenting an invented identity to the world and asking everyone to consider it worthy of their attention. You are putting your foot down and saying that you are a valuable entity in the market, and others will benefit enormously by knowing you. So even when you are just pitching a specific product or service produced by your company, you are still representing the overall identity of your brand.

In the last section, we talked a lot about how understanding your target audience is just as important as understanding yourself. Great communication is a two-way process. Whatever words you use in speech or writing need to be tailored towards the pre-existing mentality of the people who will be on the receiving end. This is part of what makes teaching so difficult. You aren't just explaining how something works. You are identifying where your student's present level of knowledge ends, and then finding the words you need to take them to the next level at their own pace and in their own way.

Everyone you pitch to will be coming from a different place, no matter how well you try to target them. You have to be very aware of the information that you are sending out and the way the people around you are predisposed to interpret different signals. Otherwise, you cannot possibly tailor your approach to them as individuals.

Some signals are universal. Basic body language is an evolved part of human psychology around the world, with only minor variations. We can even see many of these same physical communication signals in other mammals. Broad, straight shoulders and a puffed out chest displays dominance, confidence, strength and sometimes aggression. Hunched shoulders and a closed off body structure show fear, submission and general lack of security. This applies to other qualities like the tone of voice and rate of speech, though cultural expectations do start to come into play here.

Artificial factors, like clothing, are more contingent upon social setting and context. For thousands of years, those who had achieved the social ranking of 'royalty' have used their fancy garments to distinguish themselves from the lower classes. Today, anyone can adorn themselves in whatever way they want. You can create the appearance of a high-status individual simply by adopting the culturally appropriate look they use. Additional accessories, such as jewellery, watches, and cufflinks, enhance this effect.

Whatever personality traits you intentionally display through your body language, tone of voice, and clothing should be consistent with your brand's overarching personality profile, which was discussed in chapter 7. Just because a jacket, dress, shirt, tie and a set of gold cufflinks are the right approach for someone else does not necessarily mean they are the right approach for you. Your audience might be served better by a more laid-back, whimsical, or ironic set of character traits. Only you can determine how to embody the new you.

The next two chapters will cover the many dynamics of speaking and writing effectively, whether in a sales scenario or for something else related to your business. They are the primary vehicles through which we deliver our story to the world, regardless of the many changes the market goes through either culturally or technologically.

THE ART OF THE PITCH

When you understand who you are and who you are presenting yourself to, it's a good idea to put your story into an official format that will guide your prospect one step at a time, from total ignorance about your existence to being ready and willing to make their initial purchasing decision with you. A great sales pitch tells an interesting story which places your prospect as the main character overcoming big obstacles on the path to greater happiness. It is designed to address their needs—not show off your accolades.

Think of things from the perspective of your customer. If I come to you looking for a very specific solution to a problem in my life, but instead of addressing what I need you start to talk about some other aspect of your product that has nothing to do with what I want, I'm not going to see what's valuable about what you do. I'm simply going to ignore it. You have to step out of your own conception of what makes your company great long enough to tell the story that I (the prospect) want to be a part of.

The way to ethically persuade new buyers is to focus on what your audience is seeking. You accomplish this much more by listening than by talking. Get your audience to start talking about themselves, what they care about, and what they are looking for. Whether you are speaking to someone over the phone, through emails, or face-to-face, most people's favourite subject is themselves. If you give them space and prime them with the right questions, they will tell you everything that you want to know about them, but only if you have learned to actively listen.

Technology and marketplace convenience have caused most consumers today to grow lazy. More often than not, the burden will fall upon you to go out of your way to show them exactly what they want to see. They don't want to have to figure things out themselves, and they won't give you many chances to present your offer in the right context, with the right combination of words and images. You can align the value that your product provides with the perception of value somebody is looking for, and then communicate that through words and images. This is when sales start to happen easily, and without unnecessary friction.

When you pitch your company, nothing will ever be quite as good as having someone right in front of you. This setup allows you to monitor how their responses change over time as you present them with new information. They won't always come right out and tell you what they like or dislike, or what they want you to say next. If you develop prowess for observation, you will see what you need to do next, clear as day in their facial expressions, body language, and tone of voice, in addition to any specific objections they raise.

This is why live cold approaches like door-to-door sales and calling are some of the hardest but most effective ways to sell. No other approach puts you in a position to divert attention away from the entire universe of other things a person may be focused on, or to monitor their expressions in real time as you navigate your way towards a sound buying decision. A skilled observer knows how to ask the right questions and present information so that it is always addressing whatever the listener is waiting for them to say next. It keeps them engaged and the conversation flowing toward the mutually desirable goal of a purchase.

In some situations, I've had to take on the task of cold calling hundreds of potential prospects before any other major selling initiative could begin, so that I could gauge the receptiveness of the market to many different variations of presenting an offer. I was able to take what was learned from those many calls, and craft it into a core narrative and multi-tier sales approach that had already been tested in the market with a large sample size.

The point of all of this was to gather enough real-world

data from actual human responses to formulate a plan of attack that could work when applied on a larger scale.

STREET CAT MARKETING AND THE COLD APPROACH TO INSTANT SALES

A personal passion of mine is animal welfare.

Specifically, I mean caring for stray cats in poor health and rehoming them with someone who will be able to look after them permanently. Most people would think this practice is incompatible with my highly mobile lifestyle, where I often won't spend more than a couple weeks or months in one location. They think finding someone to adopt a cat is a lengthy process and not something that can be accomplished spontaneously. After all, just look at how many stray cats there are on the street or sitting in shelters waiting for owners.

Over the course of the last year, I've taken at least a dozen cats off the streets of Guanajuato, Casablanca, Kumasi, Kuala Lumpur, Ubud, Tbilisi, Athens, and other cities, and found new permanent homes for them. The reason I am equipped to do this is because I understand the art of the cold pitch. I know how to target qualified prospects from a large group of random people, show off the most uniquely attractive attributes of what I am selling, and say the right words that lead to a buying decision as quickly as possible. I can do this even in a place where I have no social connections and am unfamiliar with the local language or culture.

I call my process 'street cat marketing.' It has a dual meaning because the cats are 'street cats,' and I'm finding new homes for them through old-fashioned 'street marketing.' It usually consists of taking my latest feline companion into my arms and meandering through a populated public area, such as parks and outdoor cafe venues, to garner the attention and interest of qualified prospects (i.e. other 'cat people'). It's an irrefutable fact that anyone who likes cats will be irresistibly drawn towards a well-dressed young man carrying a cute little kitty in his arms. This is the first step in the process of qualification, and they quickly become viable leads.

The sheer unusualness of the situation causes a great many people to look my way or come right up to me to pet the cat and ask me questions. Already, I am gathering attention by being unique in my setting. Since at this point they are already intrigued and asking me questions, all I have to do is answer in a way that continues propelling them into wanting to know more. I answer in the form of a short narrative—a story about how I am a perpetual traveller living around the world, rescuing cats as I go. Now they have context, both for who I am and the critical information, which will come next.

When I explain that I found the cat I am holding struggling to survive on the street, and how eager it was to come home with me, and how it has since turned into a healthy and social pet, my audience becomes emotionally engaged. They are ready for the call to action.

I tell them that I will be leaving the country soon, and that if I can't find a new home for this cat who has risen from poverty to be the beautiful creature they see before them, whose soft fur and loving eyes they are in the process of engaging with emotionally, I will have to put it back on the street where I found it. If I really want to drive the point home, I will show them pictures on my phone of what a poor condition the cat was in when I first found it. This serves as proof of concept for the story I am telling and validates their blossoming emotional engagement.

They immediately understand, without me saying it, that the cat will lose the trust of humans it has developed and will revert to being a mangy wild animal again. At that point, I rarely even have to ask them to do anything. If they are able to take the cat themselves and give a home, they offer to. Or, more likely, they offer to search around for me to find someone who wants a cat and get back to me.

The entire exchange may take only a minute of time, but the message and its impact are clear. It has not failed me yet, and I've been able to find homes for stray cats in as little as one hour, or sometimes up to a few weeks. One even had a litter of five kittens under my care and reared them in my suitcase for six weeks until I could find someone willing to take in the whole family.

What makes this all possible is better narrative and the boldness of the cold approach that so few founders are willing to try with their own products. The cats (the 'products' in this scenario) are already there, free for the taking for anyone who comes to a conclusion on their own that they want one. The reason they don't go out of their way to take home a stray cat on their own is because no one has made it convenient for them to do so, or given them any special, unique reason to choose one cat over another.

When they are spontaneously presented with an offer using my cold street cat marketing approach, they aren't looking at the concept of adopting a stray cat as a whole. They are looking at a unique creature, which exists in a category all on its own. This enables a deeper level of emotional investment. There are elements of scarcity and urgency added to the conversation. There's only one of this particular cat with such an endearing story, and a decision must be made quickly, or the opportunity will be lost forever, and the poor little kitty will be the one to pay the price.

As a salesman, I can be the bridge that connects these potential 'buyers' with what they didn't know they wanted, until just the right offer presented itself to them. It's good for them, and it's good for the cat. Its win-win, and best of all, the whole thing never even comes across as a sales pitch. The people I speak to never get the impression they are being marketed to or manipulated into taking a certain kind of action. They just do what feels right to them in the moment.

The best sales pitch in the world is the one which is never seen.

SIMPLE VS. COMPLEX VALUE PROPOSITIONS

The simpler your value proposition, the easier it will be to communicate it to a mass audience. Conversely, the more complex the product, the more it will appeal to a specific demographic of buyers with more refined preferences. In these cases, it will be far more important to talk about the quality of its ingredients, the technique with which it's made, the expertise of the people behind it, and every other potential differentiator. As a small business owner, it is not viable for you to try to appeal to mass audiences. Your goal should be to go deep and narrow with a specific promise and make your brand synonymous with it.

For a major purchase like a car, people tend to do a lot of thinking about every detail that goes into the decision. They consider how often it might need maintenance, or everywhere they might want to drive it in the foreseeable future. How many people will you be transporting in it? How quickly should it go from 0 to 60? How safe would it be in an accident? What's the resale value after 100,000 miles? These and more are the variables which your pitch will need to address, if you want to make an impression with such a specific and complex value proposition.

How you arrive at exactly what information is relevant to your audience, and what is superfluous, depends on how good you are at asking questions and how well you listen. It's your job alone to figure out the right questions to ask the right people, as people rarely know what crucial information to share without being prompted. This is why actually engaging in conversation instead of just delivering a one-sided speech is crucial in the formation stages of your brand.

Things are very different when you try to pitch your offer in a static written format. Sales copywriting is such a valuable skill because it requires knowing which way to frame what you are selling so that it will garner the highest response from its readers. Since you cannot test and adjust a written sales pitch as it is being read, you have to take extra care in the writing and editing stages, well before it is ever published. You must anticipate what problems the readers are facing when they start reading, and how to guide their perspective one step at a time with each passing sentence to the conclusion you want them to reach.

You can maximize the effect of any written media that goes out to mass audiences by testing multiple variations in smaller sample groups first. This will allow you to identify trends in how your target market responds to different types of writing or specific selling points, and you will be much better prepared in all your future sales copywriting.

LINKING PRACTICAL VALUE AND EMOTIONAL EXPERIENCE

It's obvious that a good sales pitch needs to contain the appealing features that sets your product apart from similar options in the market. Beyond the physical facts of what makes your offer more practical than the competition, is an entire emotional spectrum of experience through which your prospects will interpret and remember your brand. Your job is to figure out how to contextualize the practical elements of what you sell with specific emotions.

It's similar to the way that we recall movies, plays, songs, and even people we have known long after the fact. When people remember a story, they think of lingering emotions which stood out in the experience—the thrill, fear, fun, or sadness they experience—more than specific plot points. These emotions colour the entire experience and set the tone of the facts and actions we witness as the viewer.

You might remember the major plot points of *Star Wars* as Luke Skywalker leaving home, learning about The Force, and destroying the Death Star. But no matter at what age you first watched it, you probably have a stronger lasting impression of the unique blend of heroism, science fiction, philosophy, space battles, and just a hint of magic that defines the 'feel' of the *Star Wars* universe. Its faithfulness to that brand feeling is what will matter in the minds of fans when deciding whether to accept any subsequent prequels or sequels as authentic successors to the originals they loved.

It is much simpler to demonstrate the practical value of your product. All you need is a technical description of what it does. If you sell herbal diet pills, it might be, 'My supplement allows women over 50 to lose 10 pounds in two weeks without dieting or exercise.' If you can't tell people exactly what meaningful benefits they will experience once they hand their money and their time over to you, you are going to have a hard time convincing them to do so. Detailed descriptions help people to get a vivid mental conception that what you are offering is what they are looking for. It removes the guesswork and risk.

In addition to the actual weight that will be lost and the specific constitution of the herbal pills you are selling, there's the way your prospect feels about weight loss. You have to take into account the potentially powerful emotions that brought them to consider using a tool to get thinner. There must be some negative emotional experience they are eager to move away from and a corresponding positive emotional experience that your product is capable of bringing to them. If you cannot accurately recreate that positive emotional state and link it to the practical features of your product, you will not be effective at selling.

Learn to think in terms of both what something does for other people and how it makes them feel. People respond to emotion before they respond to intellectual reasoning, and this is what creates engagement. However, you don't want to present empty emotions without something real to back them up. Talk about the practical benefits in terms of how your buyer will feel after using your product and relate these feelings causally to the specific features of your product. With preparation, everything can be framed in terms of how it makes the life of your buyer better.

The context of your relationship with the prospect also matters. You should be able to make complete strangers feel like they know you well enough to trust that your words are true, and their money is safe with you. You can accomplish this with a powerfully appealing personality for your brand and by showing them, you understand their problems.

PROOF OF CONCEPT

Even the most poorly worded sales pitch in the world can still be successful if it can do at least one crucial thing correctly—provide proof of concept. Proof of concept is anything which demonstrates to your audience that the claims you make are true. It can be as subtle as mentioning real examples of how your product has benefited other people in situations similar to your prospect (or even your own life). It can be as obvious as a live demo of the product itself.

If you are selling a service you will be performing yourself, are there opportunities within the sales pitch to show off the effects of the service? If you are a consultant talking to a new prospect for the first time, can you show them in the first 15 minutes of the conversation how many opportunities they aren't fully acting on, or other new ways of thinking? As you do little things like this during your first conversation, it signifies that you know what you're talking about and are worthy of the price you are asking.

To make use of proof of concept effectively, you need to be intimately aware of the dominant problem your prospect has come to you for help with. Do you know what he or she is thinking when deciding whether to buy Car A versus Car B, book this vacation package versus that vacation package, or hire you, instead of someone else, as a coach? Usually, they're looking for something specific and measurable. Figure out what it is for your prospect and find a way to show them how your product caters, accordingly.

OVERCOMING OBJECTIONS

Objections are any ideas in the mind of your prospect that may prevent him or her from making a sound buying decision. It's quite rare that you will run into people who are already certain they want to purchase what you are selling. A large majority of them will need to be convinced to some degree that yours is the best possible choice available to them and that means the burden is on you to address the spoken and unspoken objections they hold.

Remember, not everyone falls into your narrowly defined target audience. A legitimate buying objection is anything that would genuinely prevent the prospect from gaining the full intended value of your offer and, therefore, make it a bad buying decision from their subjective perspective. Maybe it is too expensive for their present financial situation. Maybe they are too busy to use it. Maybe their wants and needs are actually different than what you presumed them to be and are not relevant to the specific problem your product solves.

Whatever it is which might disqualify them, it is in the best interest of both of you to identify these things as quickly as possible so that you can stop the sales process and not waste each other's time. It would be wholly unethical of you to continue trying to sell something to someone who has displayed a legitimate objection to your offer.

If you've done your targeting well enough though, the people you try to sell to should only have minor illegitimate objections. An illegitimate objection is any reason not to buy based on a misperception about the product or an irrational emotion. If a prospect fails to see how your product will solve their problem in a uniquely superior way than any other choice available to them, it means you have failed as a communicator. It is up to you to figure out what you have to say or do to show them the unseen value of your product in an undeniable way. Only then will they put the pieces together and reach a rational conclusion about the inclusion of your product in their life.

What if their objection is emotional? Sometimes a prospect already completely understands what they stand to gain by purchasing your product. They've already assessed the risks as well as the time and monetary costs involved with saying yes to your offer. Yet, still they hesitate. They've never spent this much money on a car before. They want to get their wife's opinion before moving forward. They just met you an hour ago and feel so flustered with the idea of suddenly giving you thousands of dollars of their hard-earned money.

These situations are where you need to switch from wearing your teaching hat to your coaching hat. To be effective in sales, you have to be willing to hold their hand and walk them through the sequence of emotions which lead to a more positive outcome for them, even if it is only their own doubt that is standing in the way.

Most importantly, you must understand that people will seldom actively voice all their concerns when they know you are trying to sell them something. It is natural for some people to see a sales conversation as adversarial instead of collaborative, and part of their way of keeping bargaining chips in their own hands is to divulge as little information as possible about themselves and their needs.

If a sale isn't going smoothly, ask yourself what information you are missing about your prospect's buying motivation and potential objections. Then, get them talking. Coax the information out of them. If you let someone talk long enough, sooner or later they will tell you everything you need to know. It's only when you understand the objections specific to their situation that you can address and overcome them. This is a primary example of where entrepreneurial empathy becomes indispensable to your success.

RISK MINIMIZATION AND REVERSAL

It's easy to forget that every time we ask a stranger to spend money with us they unavoidably take a risk. You might be certain that what you are offering is the answer to your customer's prayers, but they aren't. They don't have the same level of familiarity with what you are promoting because your pitch is likely to be the first time they have ever heard of it. For that matter, you can never be 100 per cent sure that what you are offering is actually the best solution for someone else, because you don't live their life. You don't evaluate things the same way they do, and you don't know the full scope of their problems. You can only make an educated guess how they see the world based on the information they choose to present to you.

For that reason, you must be willing to take the inherent uncertainty of choice out of their hands and into your own. This happens commonly in the form of warranties, guarantees, return policies, or revisions to the work that has already been delivered. This reassures potential buyers because it gives the seller incentive to be extra sure that what they are promoting will actually deliver the results they claim, and it is actually the right fit for their specific situation.

There is a danger of making promises too big to fulfil, and unscrupulous buyers may take advantage of you if you are too generous in your claims. Contrary to popular belief, the customer is not always right. The decision to purchase anything is a contractual agreement between buyer and seller, and each has promises they are obligated to fulfil. If a buyer makes unreasonable demands about your product that you never agreed to, you are at no fault for sticking to your guns and respectfully informing them that they are mistaken in their expectations of you.

That being said, many larger brands will bend over backward to appease even customers who are clearly in the moral wrong because it is better for their public image. How far you are willing to go to stop irrational people from complaining is a policy you must be very wise about making, as you will need to stick to it throughout the life of your company. It is an important part of your brand personality. Are you going to be the company that works extra hard to make everyone happy? Or are you going to be stern and stick to your guns when you know you are right?

Whenever you present your offer to someone, make it clear that you are willing to make a reasonable effort to ensure their satisfaction, even long after the sale is complete. This is the way to turn one-off impulse purchases into long-term relationships with your brand. It makes the lifetime value of any client worth substantially more, as they will be willing to return to you months and years into the future to purchase more solutions related to their problem. They will also be more likely to promote you organically through word-of-mouth to others in your target demographic.

When you can master these principles and apply them

to all your sales efforts, you get more customers and happier customers. You get customers who will return to you often and bring their friends because you've done something for them that no one else has ever done before.

10

How to Speak with Clarity, Authority and Authenticity

Whether or not they ever aspire to be a professional public speaker, a salesman, or any other type of presenter, every entrepreneur should learn at least the fundamentals of the spoken word. Why? It is because speaking and writing are the primary ways in which we communicate value and instructions to other people.

When you speak to your team members, there is a huge range of different types of impact you can have on them, which depends on how well you communicate their roles to them and how you attempt to motivate them or build a stronger company culture. When you seek out partners and other business-to-business relationships, you will find that the willingness of other professionals to work with you will be heavily affected by how they feel when they talk to you and the conciseness with which you present information in conversation.

You may already be thinking to yourself that you'll just hire a salesperson to be the face and voice of your company when a real human presence is needed to make the right live impression, or to cold call potential buyers, or make a presentation. Even if that is ultimately the best business decision for your company to outsource its sales and/or marketing, there are many other benefits to understanding how to communicate, both as an individual and as the visionary behind your company.

We have already covered the basics of good salesmanship in **Chapter 9: How to Sell Who You Are**. We will talk more about the nuances of communication with other businesses in **Chapter 12: How to Educate Your Audience**. I'd like to take some time now to focus on the act of speaking itself, so that you will be prepared to use it well in whatever context it is called for.

These are easy techniques I have learned first-hand through many years of having to communicate slowly and clearly while explaining difficult concepts to young children or helping countless foreigners understand how to use English like a native speaker, as well as giving sales presentations and private consultations for high-dollar services.

What you say should not be arbitrarily arrived at. For efficient communication to occur, everything you say must have a point to it. There's a phrase I'm very fond of which states that 'in every conversation, someone is being sold.' That's not meant to be taken literally in the sense that every sentence out of your mouth should be for the purpose of selling a product, but rather that whatever you communicate to another human being is done so with the unspoken intention of affecting their thoughts in some way.

Do you know what the point of the conversation is before you open your mouth? If you don't, there's a very high probability that you will end up meandering aimlessly as you go, confusing your audience or diluting your message. In one form or another, your mission is to change the behaviour of another person when you talk to them.

COMMUNICATION BEYOND WORDS

As anyone who has travelled to a foreign country without knowing the local language will tell you, there's a whole lot more to communication than just understanding the words being spoken. Over the last 10 years, I've managed to make my way around most of the world, despite only speaking English and conversational Spanish.

The reason why it's even possible to function in a society where words have no meaning is that there is so much more going on. Emotions are easy to convey by smiling and talking sweetly, or conversely by furrowing your brow and yelling. Universal concepts like the size of objects, the direction where things are located, the quantity of things being discussed, or the desire to crack open a cold one with the boys can all be communicated fairly effectively through hand gestures and simple grunts.

Working as a foreign English language teacher, I encouraged the students I had who were more timid to gesticulate as much as possible when using what few words of English they knew. I wanted them to see that better communication was possible by doing very simple things well than by trying to memorize as much of the English language as possible. By getting accustomed to the basic ways of using their new English tongue from day one, they had access to a much larger range of communication possibilities, which did not depend on having a large vocabulary.

They learned to communicate without fear or second-guessing—to combine intuitive whole-body expressiveness with whatever vocabulary they had at their disposal. The result was seldom perfect, but they found themselves surprisingly capable of getting across what mattered most.

STYLE VS. SUBSTANCE IN SPEAKING

The overall impression you create every time you open your mouth will be determined by both the content and style of what you say. Style goes a very long way in creating a compelling verbal communication. The most boring information in the world can spark interest and curiosity if it is spoken in the right way. This is why voice actors make so much money. It's often their job to figure out how to put just the right emphasis on a series of words, pause at just the right times, and create the desired emotional response in a speech, story, or advertisement.

Conversely, the most interesting or important topic in the world will be utterly ignored if it is talked about in a monotonous, unconfident, or annoying tone of voice and style of speech. People are emotional creatures, and we respond intuitively to what grabs our senses boldly. Only after we are emotionally engaged do we stop to process the intellectual content that we are hearing.

Speaking style becomes even more important on the phone or through video chat applications like Skype. The person you are talking to has very little information to garner about you other than through the way you present yourself via your voice, and to a lesser extent facial and body language. A great phone call can do wonders for you, especially if your physical appearance is not as effective at creating the presentation you desire.

Sounding confident when making bold claims is crucial for having others trust you. If you master this, you can have strangers ready and willing to spend hundreds or thousands of dollars within a matter of minutes of speaking to you for the first time. The expectation is that it is difficult for a forthright person to speak with sincerity and confidence.

This is why our intuition will often alert us when someone is lying or embellishing the facts. Their manner of speaking unconsciously changes in very subtle ways, and we can detect that something is off. This is yet another reason excellent actors are paid so highly and granted celebrity status. They can make us believe anything the script demands because they can alter so precisely the emotion behind their delivery.

Besides general confidence, do you even know what type of emotions you want to be associated with your brand? This is one of the core elements of your brand's personality profile, and it should be accurately reflected in the way you speak.

BODY LANGUAGE

Many studies have come up with some surprising statistics about addressing an audience. Some experts claim that 55 per cent of the communication is via body language, 38 per cent is the tone of voice, and only the remaining 7 per cent is the actual content of your message. Whether or not these are completely accurate, the undeniable truth is that an enormous amount of how other people perceive your identity and the message you are trying to convey is determined by the way you use your body, not just the way you use your voice.

Don't let those figures lead you to the assumption, however, that the spoken message is somehow not important. That 7 per cent is still crucial. It is the whole reason why you are standing in front of another party in the first place. To get the message contained in that 7 per cent across effectively, you need the other 93 per cent to support and enhance it. Your audience needs to be receiving you on both explicit and implicit levels in order to avoid narrative incongruence in their perception of you. The misalignment between what is explicitly stated and what is intuitively perceived is often what causes us to mistrust others, even if we don't fully understand why.

No matter whom you are talking to, your body language should be natural, not forced. This is hard to describe because what comes naturally will vary from person to person. The goal is to appear comfortable to your audience, because this is what creates trust and confidence in what you are saying. If you are most comfortable putting your hands in your pocket, that is a far superior alternative to making uncomfortable gesticulations or holding them awkwardly at your sides because you read somewhere that that is what makes for good body language. The theme you've no doubt seen repeated throughout this book by now is to know yourself well and frame your actions accordingly.

If you are addressing a large group, your body language should not just be an exaggeration of the gestures you would use in a one-to-one discussion. Use eye contact with as many people as possible in the room and from audience members in all areas of the room. Don't focus on one person or one area. You will make them feel uncomfortable and everyone else will feel left out. If the format allows, move around the stage—this brings you into contact with more of your audience, and as long as you don't overdo it, it is more visually stimulating for the audience.

Your tone and body language are both things that can be taught, and learning will happen as you become more assured and confident by using the techniques below. As with anything new, you will learn faster by putting these habits into practice right away, even imperfectly.

ENGAGE WITH YOUR AUDIENCE

The success of any form of communication depends upon the engagement of the audience. People must be paying attention to you and interested in what you have to say next. You have to stimulate their natural curiosity and activate the appropriate emotions. This may be easier said than done, but there are some good, easy-to-use techniques that make this a relatively simple thing to accomplish.

Make it personal. One of the advantages of getting your message across verbally, as opposed to via the written word, is that it gives you the chance to bond or engage with the audience in a way that is impossible with emails, brochures, and other written sales literature. You have to take full advantage of this and use it. Besides using good body language and tone of voice, a very good way of doing this is to bring the message down to an emotional and personal level for whomever you are speaking to.

It is very tempting for the technically minded to present whatever they are talking about in technical terms and stay in the realm of theory. Using anecdotes, examples of things that have happened to you, your associates or friends, and telling them in a way that evokes emotion is an incredibly powerful way of getting the audience to see things from your perspective and envision how what you are talking about applies to their own life.

The emotions you tap into can be any that will serve your purpose for communicating. They can be sadness, exhilaration, grief, triumph, frustration, amusement, anger, or anything else that will get the audience to empathize with you or incentivize them to reach a specific conclusion. Opening yourself up emotionally is a very strong way of getting people to firstly listen and then to side with you. Once you have won them over, half the battle is won.

Start with a bang. Like any social interaction, the first impression is crucial. Many people will have made up their minds about you within the first few minutes of meeting you. How you begin your conversations and presentations is, therefore, one of the most important parts of the whole process. If you lose the audience at the beginning, it is unlikely you will be able to win them over from then on, no matter how strong your argument is.

The use of emotional anecdotes is one good way to start. Sometimes, a highly informative statistic or fact that is relevant to your talk works perfectly well, especially if it is something that people are unlikely to know.

If you are selling data or analysis, then this is relatively straightforward. Whatever the topic or reason for your talk, a little digging will provide some nugget of information that will make your audience sit up and take notice on both an intellectual and emotional level. You will instantly have earned their respect, and you will from then on be seen as an expert in your field (or at least someone who has something to offer).

By putting all these things together and mixing them with your own style and personality—which is something that you should never destroy by changing your approach—you will become a confident orator. The more confident you become, the more you will be able to improvise, and then everything mentioned in this chapter will become second nature. Not only will you be able to deliver knockout presentations time and time again, but you will also begin to actually enjoy and even look forward to them.

11

How to Display Your Character through Writing

Writing has become the most prevalent form of communication in the age of the internet. Just as with speaking, your *style* of writing is often more important than *what* you write. Spelling, grammar, punctuation and choices in vocabulary all contribute to the way that people interpret what you write. This doesn't mean going out of your way to use unnecessarily complex language or becoming a master grammarian. It means showing that you have put thought and intention into every detail of what you do.

Effective writing means getting the whole message across as quickly as possible without wasting words, but also without sacrificing the way you display yourself.

The two major sins of bad writing are polar opposites:

- Making something too long and complex.
- Making it too short and oversimplified.

The perfect written communication is one that tells your

audience exactly who you are, why you are talking to them, why they should care, and what you want them to do next. This is true whether you are applying for a job, soliciting business, or nearly anything else. The last thing you want to do is start a conversation with a stranger with an open-ended, ambiguous statement, or drone on about details they've never asked for.

HONING YOUR WRITTEN VOICE

The voice is something that is more often associated with fiction writing, but it is just as crucial when you're writing for business. Put simply, the voice is the style—or personality, if you like—of what is written. It doesn't as much describe what is written, but the way it is put across. It is important in business writing for two reasons.

First of all, it needs to be consistent with every piece of written and non-written communication that represents your company and brand. If your website uses short, snappy dialogue, images and ideas, this needs to be carried on through any adverts, PR, sales brochures, and elsewhere. Otherwise, your message will end up looking confused. This can be a problem if more than one person writes the copy for your company, or you have different departments, people, or agencies working on different areas. If this is the case, it is crucial they are all aware of the voice of the company before they begin.

This is a symptom of a larger problem collectively known as 'narrative incongruence,' which is failing to meet the expectations set by the character or overall personality of your brand. It is covered further in **Chapter 7: Crafting Your Personality Profile**.

Secondly, the voice has to tie in with your audience, which

brings me to the next technique—always be aware of who your audience is.

If you don't, first of all, know who your audience is, and then write with them specifically in mind, everything else is a waste of time. Your audience is the people who will actually be reading the words you have written. You need to methodically work out who this audience is by understanding who are the most qualified to purchase your product and receive the most benefit from the specific value it offers. See **Chapter 8: Knowing Your Target Audience**.

Before you begin any writing, start by asking yourself three questions:

1. Who will be reading this?
2. Where will they be reading it?
3. Why am I writing it?

Taking these questions in order, you need to know what type of person the piece is aimed at. If you are writing it for CEOs or senior managers, your language and style will be different than it would be if you were writing it for the sales team. Similarly, if it is aimed at experts in the industry, it will be completely different than one written for the man on the street. The more you understand who they are, how they live their lives, and what they care about, the more easily you will be able to write in an engaging way that will motivate them to take action and begin a relationship with your brand.

If it is a piece in a trade magazine, people will have made a specific effort to take the time out of their day to read it. If it is a flyer that will be slipped into the same magazine, you are going to have to get your point across a whole lot quicker. In the online world, there are dozens of different mediums with vastly different user experiences for their readers. The way people commonly use Facebook is different than how they read blog posts or respond to banner ads. If you don't understand the medium, you can't possibly understand how people will interpret it.

It is best to start with the writing mediums you are already familiar with and the places you already spend time reading.

When you understand clearly why you are writing it, your mind will focus on the intended outcome. What are you hoping will happen when the person has finished reading your piece? If it is a call to action, and you're hoping they will pick up the phone or click on that link, everything in your piece should point the reader toward that. If you don't know why you are writing it, you can be pretty sure that your audience won't either. Be clear on your goals from the beginning and understand how you expect new readers to begin their relationship with your brand.

STRUCTURE AND PACING IN WRITING

Whenever you set out to write anything, particularly larger articles or pieces for your brochure, website, or other written material, it is essential you have a structure in place. This goes back to our previous paragraph regarding knowing what your goals are and who your audience is, but takes it further. Great books need a start, middle, and an ending. This is just as true when writing for business or any form of non-fiction. Narratives give our brain a framework through which it can interpret new information more effectively.

Another way of looking at this, and one that may make more sense in this context, is that each piece should have an introduction, the main body of the text, and then a conclusion. They don't have to be labelled, but if you have this structure in your mind when writing, it will help to give your work a more clearly defined meaning.

1. THE INTRODUCTION

An introduction to anything gives you the opportunity to explain why you are writing your piece. This book has an introduction, which is intended to briefly explain the backstory that led to its creation, as well as an overview of what type of person will benefit most from reading it, and in what ways their life will be different as a result of making through the 65,000 words of content. It allows potential readers to qualify or disqualify themselves and generate enough interest to get started on the long journey ahead.

Your introduction will tell the reader what he or she will get from reading the next two, five, ten paragraphs or more. A good way of doing this is to introduce a problem that the reader will have experienced—the same problem that your piece of writing will address. This has the dual purpose of not only letting the reader know what the article is about, but also piquing their interest.

Be careful not to go into too much detail at this stage. This is just to whet the appetite of your audience. You have identified a problem—a need of the reader. Mention the long-term effects of this problem, ones that the reader may not even have been aware of. Do everything you can to bring home major pain points associated with this problem and the ongoing consequences of ignoring the solution you are about to give them. Very often, when we face the same recurring problem for a very long time, we grow numb to the pain until someone reminds us that it doesn't have to be that way. If you've set up your introduction correctly, your reader will now be motivated to read on to see how you can solve his or her problem.

2. THE MAIN BODY

This is the main body of the piece and where you put your point across—the reason for writing the article in the first place. This is where you put your solutions to the problem identified in the introduction. This main section will make up the majority of the whole piece and should do everything that the introduction promises it will. This is the chance to expand on the premises you set up in your introduction, educate your audience about something very valuable, and ultimately sell your services by motivating your reader to care about who you are and what you are offering.

Selling happens when people are engaged in who you are and what you are doing. The only way to create that natural reaction authentically is to talk about something people are inherently invested in. When you can connect your identity and actions to an existing interest, you can borrow the influential force already present in their mind that impels them to learn more and take action. 'The official beer of the NFL' appeals to both beer drinkers and football fans alike. It gains an instant reputation through association.

If you've done a good job tapping into the existing problems and desires of your target audience, it should not be very difficult to connect them to your brand identity or a specific product you offer. They will care about who you are, because you have associated yourself in a positive way with something that, in part, defines who they are. Use this space to create that association and build a bridge in the mind of your reader between what they have and what they want. You are that bridge.

3. THE CONCLUSION

When you have successfully introduced a problem and gone on to provide a valuable solution to that problem, the conclusion is your opportunity to wrap it up nicely—leaving the reader in no doubt about the value of what he or she has just read. The easiest way to do this is by going back to the original problem that started the whole piece off and then reminding the reader how your solution will rectify this problem. End by detailing the benefits that the reader will experience by solving this problem in a specific and compelling way that no other solution currently offers.

A common phenomenon in sales and marketing is the concept of the elevator pitch. This is a short script about your company or your product, designed to get enough information across in 30 seconds (about the amount of time you would be sharing in an elevator ride with a stranger) to make them want to know more and take specific follow-up actions. The conclusion of your writing can function very similarly to an elevator pitch. In a very short amount of time, you can summarize the original problem and the unique solution your product or company provides.

The end of a written piece is also where you are most likely to find explicit 'calls to action.' This is where you directly ask or order the reader to do something very specific that up until now has only been hinted at or suggested by the rest of the content. In some longer form sales copy, you will see many iterations of a call to action peppered throughout the page to give readers many chances to make a decision. For the best possible results, you should be very specific about what you expect the reader to do as a result of the change in awareness they have experienced by reading everything which came prior.

Do you expect the reader to make a buying decision and purchase a product from your shopping cart system right then and there? Do you want them to give you their name and email address so they can join your mailing list? Do you want them to pick up the phone and call you, or attend a specific event at a time and place? Maybe you just want them to visit your website.

By the time you get to the end of this book, you will see that my call to action is to go to my company's website (www.identitypublications.com), where you can get in touch with me about branding and book publishing, check out my other books, or learn about other ways to act on the content of this book.

Do you see how I just peppered my call to action into the middle of my written content?

FORMATTING (THE CLOTHES YOUR WRITING WEARS)

As well as being informative and entertaining enough to grab the reader's—or potential reader's—attention extremely quickly, a piece of writing needs to look attractive. Attractive writing needs to be presented in a way that is easy to grasp.

This, of course, varies widely with the intended audience and purpose of the writing. Anything intended for mass audiences is usually 'dumbed down' to be appealing to as many people as possible at the expense of depth. Newspapers and magazines are often designed to be written at an eleventh grade reading level so as not to exclude anyone or make it difficult to make it all the way through an article.

One of my own struggles as a writer has been to present my extremely rapid—and usually long-winded and esoteric—thought streams in a manner which will appeal to and educate my readers, without losing any of the substance they contain in their original form within my mind. The intended audience for this book is people who are not overwhelmed by an in-depth examination of the principles that make their business work or not. You don't have to be a genius or a marketing fanatic. You just have to want to learn and have your previous assumptions challenged in a very direct and structured way.

In fact, the tone I take with the people I work with is a crucial part of my own USP and brand personality as both a coach and an educator. It's certainly not what everyone is looking for, but to the right kind of person, it is irreplaceably valuable. Done correctly, your writing style should be one of the primary avenues through which people come to know your emotional character, as well as the practical value you offer.

Information overload also affects how we digest information and where we choose to place our attention. In recent years, we have changed the way that we look at and digest information dramatically. The advent of the internet means we now get far more information via the web than we do from traditional methods, which has made it is a lot easier for people to gloss over or even discard any written piece. This doesn't make it as easy for them to glean the information they need.

A big block of text appears intimidating and off-putting, and only someone who has actively searched out your piece will be committed enough to continue. Formatting counts for a lot in getting someone to sit down and pay attention to your words long enough to make it all the way through. That includes things like font choice, emphasis through bold and italicized phrases, numbered lists and bullet points, and the length of sentences or paragraphs.

Think of these kinds of formatting as the clothes your writing wears. Regardless of the content of his character or his skill or expertise, a well-groomed man in a nice suit is going to command a lot more respect than his equivalent in baggy jeans and overgrown hair. Unless, of course, he has strategically made those normally off-putting elements a part of his brand identity, as so many writers have done with their unconventional style (think Jack Kerouac's *On the Road*).

Writing done with the intention of getting a point across should be broken up into several short paragraphs. Bullet points are also a very good way of breaking up text. As well as making it more appealing and approachable, it makes it easier for someone to quickly cast their eyes over the information to see if it is worth for them investing more time in the piece. Typically, when anyone is faced with a page of text, they will read the title, the first few lines, and then scan the rest of the piece. If they deem it worthy of their time, they will then read it through from the beginning. That is why it is essential to have a strong opening.

Use of titles to denote subsections is a good way of breaking up the text, as well as leading the reader's eye to the places where the relevant information can be found. Being able to organize enormous amounts of information is half the battle won. Taking the example of the introduction, middle, and conclusion that we detailed before, a good title for the introduction would be the problem that you are trying to solve.

Example: *'Instant Coffee Should Taste as Good as Real Coffee'* (a major personal grievance of mine).

This is something everyone in your intended audience will recognize. It is straight to the point, and without any preamble, the reader will know what the article is about and whether it is worth their time to read. The rest of the article practically writes itself just from the title alone. The reader can already predict how the paragraphs which follow will explain how and why the taste of conventional instant coffee is terrible compared to a rich, bitter, brewed cup of coffee. They will find themselves nodding in agreement about something they had previously accepted as unavoidable without room for improvement. Once the reader is in that state of mind, they will be very open to the suggestion of trying a new brand of instant coffee that promises to match or exceed the taste of brewed coffee. If such a product were on the market with the right storytelling prowess behind it, I promise it would be an overnight success.

The title for the main body of the writing is a good way of introducing your product or service, while the title for the conclusion could be the main benefit gained from using the product in the second title, to solve the problem in the first. It could also be the call to action itself, such as *'Add Our Instant Coffee to Your Morning and Experience the Difference.'*

Finally, a very powerful way to get your argument across is to use real life examples. You don't have to name specific names, but relating the initial problem, the solution you are able to provide, and then statistics and hard facts from the results achieved make it appear all the more real. It would elevate it in the mind of the reader from some drawing board theory to something tangible that the customer and potential customer could visualize as applying to themselves.

Confused yet? Every guideline presented here has its appropriate time and place for use. They are meant to work well for *most* people *most* of the time. There are exceptions to every rule, and only through experimentation, and knowledge of both yourself and your market will you find a unique combination of different writing traits that works optimally for you. The first and most important rule to every facet of brand identity is knowing yourself.

12

How to Educate Your Audience

The greater the meaning behind your business, the harder it becomes to communicate it to the world. A complex idea or deep ideology cannot be spammed out to the masses in the same way that a sexy model eating a cheeseburger can. You can post positive affirmations against a kitten backdrop all day on your Twitter feed, but what are you actually accomplishing for your business by doing so? The majority of entrepreneurs who take this approach do so because they need to feel like they are getting something done and don't know any other path to take.

Education marketing is a high-friction approach to gaining traction with a particular audience. It consists of producing content that is very dense in informational value and that by itself already provides its readers with proof of the concepts behind your business. It brings marketing down to the real world and away from the cartoon imagery of most popular ad campaigns. Education marketing is how real businesses display what they can offer to the world.

It's not always immediately obvious how you can turn your business into compelling educational content. It takes expert attention to uncover what your audience is most interested in learning about, and gradually to craft the voice through which you will deliver this pressing information. Teaching itself is a skill that must be learned through attention and repetition, regardless of how well you understand your subject or your technical skill in any domain. To put a new spin on an old saying, 'Those who do, cannot necessarily teach.'

Education is about explaining difficult concepts in simple terms. The power of education marketing to bring widespread viral attention within a niche group of prospects is enormous. For certain types of businesses, it is nearly the only type of marketing that has any real influence on the number of paying clients you accrue with each new implementation. Getting someone's attention with superficial content is not enough to close sales on a high-end or highly niched enterprise, and you will need to be bold enough to think in more mature terms than 99 per cent of the other guys out there who are fighting for attention in the market.

No matter what the physical component of your business consists of, there is always room for expansion through education. Most importantly, education is infinitely scalable and isn't weighted down by the constraints of physical production and distribution, if you make use of digital education methods.

THE OLD SCHOOL MODEL OF COERCIVE SALES TACTICS

The old school method of selling relies on identifying a very specific pleasure or pain point in a prospect's life and agitating it to an extreme. If your target is a man in his early twenties seeking a girlfriend, the most effective approach would be to take the initial unhappiness he felt about being single. Then, to blow it out of proportion until he saw it as an all-consuming fear of being alone for the rest of his life and having all his peers look down on him for being such a loser.

We've all seen the overly dramatic simulations featured on infomercials, where actors portray ordinary people with minor problems which are suddenly ruining their entire lives. Can't use a blanket without losing the use of your arms? Oh, the humanity! There's a product for that. Can't cook a simple meal without covering your entire kitchen in food? You bet there's a product for that.

On the opposite end of the spectrum, the old school salesman wants to make you believe that your life will be endlessly amazing, better than you ever possibly could have imagined, once you purchase his solution. You were lonely and worthless before you bought his dating system, and now every day is a waking state of nirvana, as women fight for you left and right the moment you leave your house. Men everywhere are envious of you. You've finally cracked the code to limitless joy, and it only took three easy payments of $199.95.

Family mealtimes will never be the same once you add your 400th novelty kitchen doohickey to your drawer. You'll finally have that perfect happy family and feel fulfilled as a housewife, but only if you complete your order in the next 10 minutes. Hurry, before this offer is banned from the internet!

These hyperbolic stories are designed to get you to feel very strongly for but a brief moment, and in that moment make the decision to spend a large sum of money on something you might otherwise have second thoughts about. The last thing the old school marketer wants you to do is rationally analyse whether or not his product deserves a meaningful place in your life —whether both the monetary cost involved and the amount of time you will have to invest into using it justify the end result for the foreseeable future.

These products aren't outright cons. Most of them do indeed perform the function claimed by their advertisements and lengthy sales pages. They are just exaggerated through artistic license and stretched to the limit of what could still be considered truthful. They are meant to take you out of your analytical mind and keep you locked into an emotional decision-making state. Act now; ask questions later.

While these borderline coercive sales tactics may produce sales, their potential is limited. They work best with very simple value propositions that can be represented by a basic emotional state in a matter of minutes or less. They appeal to lazy people who don't put a lot of thought into their purchasing decisions or the best way to go about solving their problems. It's not just price that is an issue, as even items costing tens of thousands of dollars, such as cars, have been sold using these old-school emotional tactics. It's about how elaborate and personal the change in a person's life will be if they choose to purchase what you are selling.

The more differentiated you are from your competitors and 'mainstream' versions of the products you represent, the more thought a prospect should put into whether or not your offering is the best possible choice for them as an individual. Though more work may be required initially to convince them to become your client, these are also the same people who will become diehard fans with unparalleled loyalty to your brand. If they are happy with the service you offer, in their mind no alternative will come close to the specific type and level of satisfaction your company creates for them.

Can you think of any products or services in your own life where this applies? Is there a brand of chocolate you crave above all others? Is there a model of acoustic folk guitar that creates a special synergy with your playing style and voice, which no other guitar on the market will ever compare to? Do you have a favourite hairdresser who understands your look and style better than any mere mortals masquerading as professionals?

If you have this kind of special connection to any product, service, or brand in your life, then you already know you would pay many times above the industry average to get the results that only your personal favourite can provide. This is how powerful client relationships are formed, and they must be strong enough to surpass any momentary emotional surges. They must stand up to the harshest analytical scrutiny in the mind of your buyer.

In general, the harder it is to win a customer's patronage, the more loyal they will remain through thick and thin. They will forgive minor errors and inefficiencies. They will be willing to pay higher prices due to higher subjective value. They will also organically spread your unique brand identity through authentic word-of-mouth marketing, which is a method of communication that no marketing budget could ever replicate.

EDUCATING YOUR AUDIENCE

For a highly personalized approach to selling to work, your audience needs to understand what they want. Part of your job is helping them figure that out. This is the educational element of sales that so many 'coffee is for closers' types ignore. They believe their job is to get someone to make a buying decision as quickly as possible or else terminate the conversation and move on to the next prospect.

There is a time and a place for the hard sell approach. It is usually most appropriate when a prospect already has all the information they need to make a sound decision but is held back only by emotional uncertainty. That is when bringing the hammer down can help others to help themselves by making the right decision. If you haven't already laid the groundwork of sound decision making prior to that point, pushing an uncertain customer to spend money just makes you a bully who is only interested in increasing his own profits at the expense of others.

Your target audience might approach the buying process thinking they already know what they want, based on what is generally available. Maybe other generic products offer enough of a solution that they have stopped looking for something better. They aren't actively asking the questions that you have the most compelling answers for. In this situation, even the best information, backed up by the strongest promises in the world, will fall on deaf ears. How do you instigate curiosity among a group of people who don't think they have any reason to care who you are?

One of the reasons I excelled as an educator, even to children who had had great difficulty learning a subject before, is that I gave all my students a reason to care about what I was trying to teach them. I understood that emotional engagement was necessary before they would be willing to put in the mental effort required to change their understanding of something. Changing ideas is hard work, and it tends to get harder the older we get. Only people who want new ideas are the ones who successfully acquire them.

This is the part of the sales process that the old school salesmen do so well. They give you a quick and powerful reason to pay attention to what they are going to say next. Where you will differ is that you will turn that engagement into a compelling lesson about why your target audience is not completely fulfilled in the domain of life that you cater to. You will help them to see that there are other ways to live, but only if they know how to make use of the right tools and expertise available. It is only after you've painted a very clear picture of what the problem is, and the potential positive alternative, that you should even consider pitching your product.

If you lead with the product itself, very few people will have the requisite information to see its unique and personal value in their life.

B2B VS. B2C COMMUNICATION

Communicating your new brand identity won't just be limited to customers. As your business grows, it will become strategically advantageous, if not outright necessary, for you to collaborate with other businesses and even potential investors. The organizations you work with might be in the same market niche or they may be in something different but tangentially related. They may even be someone who you previously thought of as your fiercest competition. If you can get them to see what the specific value your brand brings to the table, there is always the possibility of a mutually beneficial partnership. For that reason, you have to know how to talk to other businesses.

The main difference between B2B (business-to-business) and B2C (business-to-consumer) interactions is that consumers want what you produce itself, whereas potential partners want to either make or save money because of what you produce. The health of their own business is always at the forefront of a business owner's concerns. To be successful in your negotiations with them, you will need to position your own organization as the key to minimizing losses, expanding gains, or otherwise increasing their efficiency.

While both audiences have a 'what's in it for me' approach to what you are offering (as all people continually seek to improve their own happiness), you will need to make major changes to your communication strategy. Businesses are interested in quality products and services that will please their customers, improve their standing in the community, and consolidate their bottom line. If they choose to promote your brand, or have themselves promoted by yours, they don't want customers complaining that your products are not living up to the standard of quality they expect. They need to feel confident that you will provide them with something that will enhance their reputation and lessen the stress of running a business.

Businesses put in a lot of time and effort into streamlining their buying process in order to cut down on time and money costs. This is why B2B purchasing is more logic based, rather than emotion based. If you want to get your widget featured on the shelves of a local retailer, the person in charge of making purchasing decisions must determine if the product or service is right for the business and their consumer base. They should not be taking into account whether your product appeals to them aesthetically or emotionally when market data is there to support the decision.

B2B marketing should inform the purchaser how your product can help or entertain their customers. It is not only about reselling a product but also about reselling an idea or emotion which they will want to pass on. The knowledge you supply them with will give them confidence in you. B2B marketing is as much about assurance and conviction, as it is about the product. For another business to take on your product, there needs to be a reliable level of trust.

Supermarket chains are full of someone else's products. While the larger ones have their own lines, a great deal of the stock is supplied by other businesses. These businesses also market directly to the customer but expect they will go to a 'middleman' to purchase it—the supermarket. The producers supplying products to supermarkets may think that having their lines in a venue where hundreds of people shop is an advantage. Even if their product is sitting alongside a competitor's, it is still being exposed.

This saves the businesses a lot of money as they do not have to set up their own shops or marketing to prospective clients. As consumers, we would think it strange to have separate shops for many of the product lines that supermarkets carry. Can you imagine a toilet paper shop or a shop that just sells milk or toothbrushes? Supermarkets will present a product to prospective customers using a variety of different techniques for maximum results. They might lower the cost, or create a special stand, or put the product in a certain place where it will attract more attention.

There is a complex level of trust here. Supermarkets don't have the time to test and trial products, and suppliers have to trust that their products will be displayed with the same impartiality as everyone else's. Either way, the customer is the winner. They can use their buying power to validate a product and frequent a certain store.

When you try to convince these middlemen to use their

limited shelf-space to feature your line of products instead of a competitor's, you need to put yourself back into that same educative sales mentality you should be using with consumers. The only difference in this situation is the concerns you will be addressing and knowledge of unknown opportunities you will be imparting.

If you were talking to a consumer, you would want to know what problems they were facing. These would be related to the use of the product. For the business owner, you will need to address how allowing your products to take up that valuable space will create higher revenue through repeat business and brand loyalty.

Will they be the only store in town that carries your high-end product, forcing your already dedicated following to shop there if they want to get their fix? Or is their store taking a gamble by letting some unknown, untested, newcomer compete against proven sellers? The more you understand the business model of the retailer and their existing customer base, the more compellingly you can structure your proposal.

In that sense, B2B marketing is a higher level concept than B2C marketing. Selling to a consumer is about creating and catering to demand. Selling to another business is about proving demand exists, and you are in a position to fulfil it. One must come before the other, unless you are dealing with someone willing to take a risk on an untested product.

INVESTOR PITCHES THAT ATTRACT PARTNERSHIP AND CAPITAL

If you ever approach an investor looking for an injection of capital in your budding business, similar rules will apply. You need to alter your standard sales approach to address the concerns of someone who may risk a lot of money on your venture. A great investor pitch is about telling your story in a way that makes the happy ending for their investment seem inevitable. Your company is the hero, and you're inviting others to join you on your journey toward victory. Like any other type of sales pitch, it must be humble, educational, and honestly address realistic obstacles before they become major issues.

When creating your investor pitch, you will have to build up a solid and convincing story about what you are promoting. The quality of the product, its production costs, and its marketing needs are all crucial factors that wise people will consider before giving up their hard-earned money. You need to be able to show that your brand has a unique identity that stands out from whatever is already available in your niche. Investors must see that there is a solid plan for connecting your uniqueness to what a specific sector of the market is looking for.

There will always be areas where your business could encounter stumbling blocks or even fail. These are the objections you must pre-emptively overcome in the minds of investors before they can ever be the cause of significant doubt. Investors are going to want to know how you plan to deal with them. What emergency tools and strategies do you have in place? Who is going to be responsible if things don't go according to your projections? What safeguards do you have to keep stumbling blocks from permanently damaging your business?

So, when you are approaching investors, it is a good idea to test all parts and sections of what you are offering. Not only will you be more confident, but they will see that you have attempted to cover every obstacle or hindrance that it is within your power to do so. No investment is more attractive than a vehicle with its path already laid out before, needing nothing more than a little gas to move it along toward its inevitable destination. The investor is simply the one providing that necessary propulsion.

SECTION IV

BRAND IDENTITY CASE STUDIES

Introduction to Brand Identity Case Studies

To better help you understand how the principles of better brand identity and communication can transform a business, I wanted to give you the opportunity to hear stories of change directly from the mouths of other entrepreneurs. Each of the following five cases involves talented individuals, from a variety of backgrounds, whom I saw undergo impressive developments in the time we worked together. I keep in touch with each of them regularly and am continually inspired by how much I've seen them grow from when I first met them.

Each case study begins with a brief introduction from me explaining the context of our working relationship and the place each business owner began their journey at. It outlines the major obstacles they were facing, irrespective of how much success they had already accomplished up until that point.

Anastasiya Plushenko had dealt with an influx of entrepreneurs whose brand messages were inconsistent across different online platforms. Laura McGregor was intent on planting seeds in the minds of both buyers and sellers with her upcoming B2B marketplace. Chris Reynolds didn't understand how to make the humanitarian projects he organized in his free time attractive enough to ensure their financial stability. Niedra Gabriel had been using the same generic elevator pitch for over 30 years and needed a drastic new way to make herself sound uniquely valuable to strangers. Olivier Wagner was reluctant to bring his own face and personality into the mix with his previously analytical approach to his expert services.

Some were just experimenting with new ideas. Some had already found an impressive amount of financial success with their past strategies. But the common theme with each is that they were failing to live up to their full potential, because they weren't completely embracing their identity and ideal way of communicating.

After each case study introduction, you'll hear directly from the mouths of the entrepreneurs themselves how they worked to overcome their problems and what difference it made for their business. Though their stories are varied, the lessons they learned are universal. Look for the common ground and see what you can apply in your own life, now or in the future.

If you want to see the results of these individuals putting their new knowledge into action, you can learn more in the Brand Identity Breakthrough online course (instructed by yours truly) at www.brandidentitybreakthrough.com/course.

Case Study #1

Unifying Brand Meaning Across Every Domain

FEATURING ANASTASIYA PLUSHENKO OF EXEMPLI AGENCY

Anastasiya Plushenko is the logistical mastermind behind Exempli Agency, a complete branding ensemble composed of experts in graphical design, website development, and online marketing. She and her colleagues work to help clients find consistency in their branding across all mediums for synergistic influence and rapid growth among their target audience. Read on to find out more about their approach to the underlying principles of good branding.

INTRODUCTION

A major problem with new entrepreneurs who are beginning to follow their passions in business for the first time is finding consistent meaning and emotion in the way they present themselves. Sometimes, it's a consequence of having too much to say and not knowing the best way to break it down to the most important elements. At other times, it is lacking awareness and proficiency in the many mediums a brand shows up in as a function of the digital age.

Anastasiya Plushenko grew keenly aware of this problem in her work as a web analyst and social media manager. She would frequently be approached by clients with large marketing budgets to blow on Google pay-per-click (PPC) ad campaigns and other venues. Yet, when they would tell Anastasiya the strategy they wanted to use, and what they were hoping to accomplish for their brand through the ads they were paying her to run, things didn't always add up.

More often than not, the message they wished to use on ad copy was vague and not compelling, or else it did not match what was already clearly stated in their website content. Even though her clients had hired her to perform a specific task related to their advertising, she found that she could not proceed unless they were willing first to take a few steps backward and reconsider some of the premises behind their message.

Many creative agents today are tasked to build something amazing atop a weak foundation. No matter how skilled they are within their specific field, they can only be as effective as the context in which they are working and the instructions they are given. When entrepreneurs lack clarity and consistent meaning in their brand, it will show up in the finished product of everything the brand produces. Anastasiya saw a big problem that was being overlooked, even among relatively successful businesses, and so she decided to combine her insight with that of other branding professionals whose skills and abilities complemented her own. That is how Exempli was born.

Exempli is a full-service branding agency designed to solve the problems and answer the questions related to creating a unique, meaningful brand. Combining logic and aesthetics, they create messages that speak in a unique manner to the hearts and minds of their clients' audiences. In order to do this, they needed to position themselves as something far beyond an ordinary creative agency. The team behind Exempli had to show passionate entrepreneurs that they were capable of building an effective brand message from the initial philosophy behind the company and then implementing that message in whatever formats would be most effective for their goals.

Read Anastasiya's tale of evolving from creating advertising messages in isolation to working in conjunction with other experts to engineer whole brands from scratch. Then think of how the principles of consistency apply to your own entrepreneurial project.

- Are you sending mixed messages to your audience through your words or design choices?
- How many assumptions do you make about the way your brand is perceived?
- Are you working to understand the needs of your audience before you solidify your message?
- Do you outsource your branding to too many different creatives, each with their own interpretation of your work?

READ ANASTASIYA PLUSHENKO'S STORY

'A good brand needs consistency. When people try to create

their own brand though, they like to split it up into separate tasks handled by different specialists. For example, one person does the graphic design for their logo, their business cards, and their brochures. Then, another person builds their website. Finally, a third person handles the online marketing, like managing social media profiles and ad campaigns.

The consistency of their brand is lost from the start. They sacrifice their core message. You cannot create a brand only with the design. You cannot create a brand only on a website layout and some social media accounts. You need everything to work together. This idea of consistency is what brought the three of us together so that we could find synergy in our strengths.

Exempli Agency began very simply. Two other women living and working across Europe and I would frequently combine our respective specialties when any one of us had been hired for a branding job that went beyond the scope of what we could do alone. My friend Nadiya was an experienced graphic designer who brought a unique look to everything from logos to business cards and even book covers. My friend Mariya was an experienced writer for all forms of content and copy. I had a diverse background in advertising and analytics. Each one of us worked well on our own, quietly doing great work in our respective domains.'

WORKING TO BUILD CONSISTENCY WITH BRANDS

'When a client comes to us with nothing, first we start with market analysis, target audience analysis, and competitor research. Then, we get into the owners' conception of what the brand represents, its market strategy, and name. Then we move on to design, then the website, and only after all that is done do we start to handle promotion.

Nadiya, the designer on the Exempli team, had previously built her own design team. When clients would come to them, they would have almost no brand elements to work with. They had no logo, no colours, or any other branding guidelines to work from. As a result, her team would create these essential branding guidelines and ultimately the whole visual core of the brand. Clients liked their work, but when they were done the clients still wanted help adapting the meaning of the new philosophy into the rest of their brand. They did not know what to do next.

In my case, clients would come to me for promotion with their logos and websites prepared, but I would see that the website didn't work the way it should. It was usually difficult to understand the message of the website and perform critical actions. I had to suggest to them to redo almost everything about their sites. If I drive traffic to a website, the website needs to be set up to sell. Otherwise, the advertising I oversee is wasted. Advertising just helps people find out about a product, but when people come to a landing page that confuses them or doesn't work, they don't connect with the brand.

Each of us with Exempli studied branding, advertising, and public relations. Mariya, our copywriter who focuses on creating brand story, concept, and social media, works with many of the biggest restaurants, bars, and nightclubs in Eastern Europe to create branding strategies from scratch. She has helped them figure out how they could be different in their highly saturated markets. Now they have this consistent story, this consistent narrative, with consistent language everywhere on their website copy, on their social media network, and on their advertising copy.'

BRAND CONSISTENCY IN THE DIGITAL AGE

'In the digital age, each message sent out by a company or individual can be different. On social media, some people post 10 times per day. You have a lot of information moving. People are very engaged and there's so much noise in media. If you don't have a unique voice, you are lost in that noise. Consistency is more important now than ever. You have to use the same branding colours, the same phrases, and the same style for a brand.

When a person scrolls down, they're so busy with their newsfeed that they never read every post that shows up. But they can easily recognize things even if they don't read the post. They can spot when something belongs to a specific brand, to a personality, to a product, and that's what branding is about: being consistently recognizable. If entrepreneurs don't have a clear vision from the beginning, they never attain this consistency.'

PROBLEMS WITH PEOPLE DOING THEIR OWN BRANDING

'Everyone has an idea in mind when they start their business. They understand what it is supposed to be about. They might start a restaurant thinking that they want it to be fancy, with a very formal interior design, etcetera, etcetera. Then, at some point down the road, they might decide they want it to appeal in a more informal way. They want patrons to come, be comfortable, and feel at home. This new desire now contradicts with the high-end, luxurious design. It doesn't work. You have already lost the consistency of your brand.

So, because our clients have their momentary preferences,

they want to try many things and move in many directions. They can't easily look at the big picture like we can. People who can't look at the bigger picture will be inconsistent. It won't work. That's why we write down and map out the brand concept before we begin any work. The brand map is a document of the core concept of the brand where we determine exactly how you will appeal to your audience. It's not enough that you like your business if you don't take these steps. Your audience will be confused. You will be lost as a brand.'

BRANDING A BRANDING AGENCY IN A UNIQUE WAY

'The Exempli Agency philosophy is based on linking design with meaning. There should always be a very strong connection. Beauty should not be empty. We started with the idea of the simplest possible display of a concept: a single dot. A dot is the beginning of everything, even before something one-dimensional like a line. Before you do anything, before you write anything, before you draw anything, you start with a dot. It is the first touch of everything.

It was difficult to come up with a meaningful name, because many design themes have been used already by other creative agencies. It was very difficult to find our own style, because each branding agency is trying to get creative, to be outstanding, and extraordinary. We, however, intentionally don't use the word 'creative.' We're trying to eliminate it because for us it's not only about creating beautiful things. For us it's about finding the best concept that will work for a brand, that it will fulfil its mission. That was difficult to come up with our own brand because of so much noise out there.

For most designers, it's all about appealing to aesthetics, to be beautiful, but for us it's also to be functional. We are all about the whole picture, from A to Z. Everything goes back to unity, beauty and meaning. So, if you look at our logos and our work, the whole philosophy's intact. It can be very simple or it can be very fancy. It depends, again, on the business of our client.

Because we cater directly to businesses, we are ultimately selling to the customers of our customers, not our customers themselves. We try to appeal to the target audience of our entrepreneur clients because, frequently, the client and their audience have different preferences. In all the branding work we do, we start by running surveys with the people who are in our clients' target audience to learn what their subjective experience has been and what they prefer. At least 80 per cent of the time, the story we hear from the customers is noticeably different than the story we hear from the entrepreneurs.

One of our biggest struggles is when we have a client who has a bloated ego about what they think will work for their brand, no matter what our research shows us. Your ego is a good thing. We value your opinion and your views. But if you're smart and humble enough, you will defer to the opinion of your target audience, as they are the ones who will be paying you.'

POPULARIZING A UNIQUE IDEA IN A NEW MARKET

'To give you an example of what I mean when I talk about consistency and completeness... Not long ago, CrossFit was a brand new concept for people. We ended up working with a lot of people in the CrossFit area, as it was rapidly growing popular. The challenge became to convey to customers what this new trend was in relation to something they already understood, such as going to the gym. Why should they care about this new trend? We decided to tease people by coming up with a character with a body made of stone which represented the power you get from CrossFit. The main appeal of CrossFit was all about having this powerful body.

After that, everything was built around this concept of stone and a powerful, sculpted body. Before even explaining what the image was all about or introducing the stone-bodied character, the CrossFit company could tease it with their branding. They didn't have to explain exactly what it was, but just show imagery. In this case, it was a logo made of stone, proclaiming that they would be opening soon. So, no one in the city where they were located understood what the campaign was all about, but young people, especially on social media, became interested and began to engage in online discussions about what they were seeing.

No money was put into paid advertising or social media promotion. Everything was spread organically just by teasing it. The people involved in the project made branded phone cases and showed them around the city where people walk. Everywhere, they had people dedicated to the idea of spreading the imagery from social media to real life for basically free. When CrossFit was finally opened, the people were already prepared to receive it. They instantly understood what it was and how they could use it to sculpt their bodies and be powerful. Now, it's the most successful CrossFit facility in the city.

If I could give any advice to business owners who are considering rebranding themselves or new entrepreneurs who want to get everything right from day one, I would say to take a lot of time to reflect on why you are really doing what you are doing with your company. If you need help figuring this out, there are always professionals you can turn to who specialize in understanding a brand's deeper meaning. Only after you have done that should you start thinking about the tangible ways your brand will show up in the world, like design, websites, advertisements and more. Then you can work with all these elements logically and sequentially in a holistic manner that greatly enhances your memorability.'

Case Study #2

Pre-Seeding a Two-Sided Marketplace for Launch

FEATURING LAURA MCGREGOR OF COMMISSION CROWD

Commission Crowd is an integrated platform for connecting commissioned sales agents with the companies looking to hire them, and for making managing their working relationship easy. Whether you are a sales agent looking for big opportunities for representing new products, or a company looking for a performance-based sales team, you can learn more about this first-of-its-kind platform at: www.commissioncrowd.com

INTRODUCTION

Laura McGregor had a problem that highly ambitious entrepreneurs everywhere are well aware of. She and her co-founders had set their sights on a very large vision and were suddenly realizing it was going to take a lot of careful tactics and highly specific messaging to reach it.

Commission Crowd's mission was to function both as a job board and a complete backend system for managing the relationships of commissioned sales agents and companies. Aside from the technical complexities of bringing this all together under the same platform, Laura had another problem that is common to businesses which work by connecting different types of people together. She had to learn how to present the enormous value that Commission Crowd offered to two different types of people, with totally different goals, simultaneously.

Maybe it's a dilemma you know very well. If you've got both buyers and sellers coming to you, you probably won't want to speak to them in the same way because their goals are different. In situations like this, you don't want to give up individualized approaches to communication entirely. You need a core messaging strategy so strong that it accurately conveys your value enough to everyone, and they will easily be able to self-identify as part of your target market. It takes a little more planning and finesse to pull off, but the results, when done right, can be huge.

By learning when to unify and when to separate her messaging, Laura was able to build an impressive registered user list for both sides of the equation well before launch, ensuring that there was a thriving community of activity going on from day one and that neither side was left wanting for more. Now that those crucial first launch steps have been surpassed with flying colours, Laura and the Commission Crowd team are able to look freely towards the future and think about scaling their initial success orders of greater magnitude.

- How many types of customers do you need to appeal to with your messaging? Is it possible to unify them under a single voice?
- How do you offer enough proof of concept through your messaging that prospective clients are willing to opt in, even before the product is ready?
- What can you do to generate a hungry audience well before your product is available for sale? What's your core message and minimum viable product?

READ LAURA MCGREGOR'S STORY

'Commission Crowd is a marketplace that connects commissioned agents with companies that want to work with them. It allows you, for instance, to connect with an agent or a company and then gives you the tools to be able to manage those relationships better.

For us, the biggest struggle is that we're building a two-sided marketplace and what that means is that we must communicate twice on everything that we do. So, our messaging must relate not only to one side, but also the other side, but then also an over-encompassing message for both. So, it's a little bit like the moment they land they need to know, they need to identify with themselves and then find out what we do in order to see what side of the equation they fit into.

Eventually, after looking at it together long enough, we were able to sort of say, "Okay well, these are all of the features and benefits of what both sides of the marketplace get." But we really needed to streamline that process and message to say, "Great, well what does that mean for each side of them, for both people altogether?"

A year ago, we knew exactly what we were building. We understood the functionality for each side of the marketplace, but we didn't really understand how to communicate. Then we decided to bring on a VIP early launch strategy as well. So, we needed help communicating the benefits of joining early. Ultimately, what we were trying to do is kind of really revolutionize an industry as well.

A lot of the solutions right now that exist within the paid performance industry for selling are very outdated, and there's also an education level that we're trying to incorporate into what we're doing. Because of that, it's challenging because sometimes people don't know that this kind of a solution could work for them as well. Our biggest challenge was to make that as broad as possible but also educational and direct. Companies needed to get a better feel for what Commission Crowd could bring to their business.'

SPEAKING TO BOTH MARKETS WITH A UNIFIED VOICE

'Now we have much better idea of the principled message we need to be sending to our audience. We want to challenge our messages constantly, and what we're finishing now is a revised version of our current website. We always need to add more clarity, but we also want to test that messaging. The most important thing is not just saying something once. It's about, like all marketing is, testing it. What works best for your target? We don't really care what we say, if the people that are hearing it relate to it and then, can act quickly, it is working.

What I think is quite phenomenal about Commission Crowd is that we launched our product with a completely seeded community because of how clearly we were able to reach out to people. Based on our overhauled messaging strategy, we were able to get 103 paid users on the company side when we opened our doors. To create income from not even having a product is sensational if you can understand that. It really says something about the strength of our messaging.

And on the sales agent side of things, some of them even waited a year to get in. Our messaging there helped us to create 465 sales agents who also seeded the system at the time of launch. So, on day one we already had a great starter community with almost five agents per company. We're finding that because of that enormous head start, we're leaps and bounds ahead of most web fast start-ups. Most are so worried in the early stages of their launch whether they'll have enough customers to prove that the idea works. We already had proof of market viability.

It was so important to us because without that immediate proof it would be too hard because two-sided marketplaces are hard enough already. We couldn't have started with something that wasn't already seeded. Otherwise, the supply and the demand were both going to be upset and leave. We needed to ensure that when they did come in that there was something to look at. The main focus for why people come to us is to connect with sales agents, but what will keep them with us is the additional functionality that allows you to manage your sales agents.

When they come to Commission Crowd, they know they want to connect with a sales agent, so that's not what they need to be educated about. The education piece is the additional pain that they don't initially think of, because there's never been a solution to help manage their sales team. There's a lot of pain in their business. They just don't think about that in terms of requiring a technology solution, because they have workarounds. They have band-aids all over their business to help them do that already, but nothing that streamlines that whole process. We had to learn to how to have a conversation that no one else was having.

They get it once you ask them, "Have you ever had a hard time managing five sales agents at one time, and understanding where they all are at in terms of their training and on boarding process with your company?" They know that at that moment they've got a PowerPoint spreadsheet, and they've got a girl who checks it every morning, and they've got this workaround that is a hassle, and it's awful, but they don't think that a solution will be out there for them.'

A FANTASTIC PRE-SEEDED LAUNCH TO SECURE THE FUTURE

'Since we've had such a successful pre-launch and launch phase, our next step is to get as quickly as possible to a product/market fit, which for us is at least 40 per cent of our user base saying that they absolutely love our product, and they would hate to be without it. As soon as we get there, we'd like to launch into Beta, and then scale really quickly because once it's out into the world, there will be competitors right behind us. For us, it's about revolutionizing the commissioned sales industry.

Our biggest challenge has been that the technology is just non-existent. The industry itself is over 100 years old, so paid performance is not new. So many companies don't think of themselves as being a good candidate for commissioned sales agents when, in reality, any business could potentially be appropriate, if you know you've got a good product and you're reputationally sound.

There's a real opportunity here for any agent to make money, and what I mean by that is that you don't just sell eBooks for $9.99. There has to be some kind of scalable income that can come from it. Our job is to kind of push out an educational piece to all markets, so that every business owner and business of any size with a great idea, a great product, and a great reputation could really get on board and use Commission Crowd.

And we've got a whole other side of the problem, which is that the commissioned sales industry, from the perspective of agents, is incredibly fragmented. For over 100 years, everybody has been calling themselves all sorts of different things. You've got "manufacturer agency." You've got "commercial agency." You've got "independent agency." You've got "self-employed agent." I can give you a list of almost 73 different job titles that we've identified that all mean essentially "paid on performance," and so it's really about trying to touch all of those people to let them know that the solution exists for them and it's free for sales agents.

We want them to be able to do their jobs better, and faster, and easier, and save time so that they can have better relationships with their company principles as well. What often happens is that sales agents will work with more than one company at a time. Imagine you're a sales agent and you've got six different companies that you're representing and for which you have to give activity updates on everything that's happening within your pipeline. So, every time that you make a call to somebody, you're updating them on some information, and every time you update a principle, you're taking time away from selling.

Essentially, Commission Crowd is an integrated CRM system. A company has their own CRM, and the sales agent has their own CRM, and when you connect them, they can manage their relationship easily. Every time you raise a lead on behalf of that company that you worked for, that company principal receives a high-level update, so no longer does the company need to feel like they must micromanage their external sales team, because now they've got the information that they really want.

They know exactly how their agent is working. What does that mean in terms of forecasting for my business? What does my pipeline actually look like? They can get back to running their business, and their sales agents are free to focus on selling.'

Case Study #3

Turning a Charity Project into a Profitable Movement

WITH CHRIS REYNOLDS OF THE ONE EFFECT

Chris Reynolds is a world-travelling digital nomad who organizes co-living spaces in exotic locations around the world for location independent entrepreneurs, as well as charitable adventure travel trips that benefit everyone involved. You can learn more about his trips to save the world at www.theoneeffect.com and other projects at: www.theentrepreneurhouse.com

INTRODUCTION TO CHRIS

What entrepreneur has never wondered, what it would take to turn their philanthropic passions into real business models? Very often, we are forced to face the false dichotomy of doing something for either love or money, but never both. For most people, it's hard enough figuring out how to make money doing anything at all, let alone the one thing which is most personally fulfilling to them.

Chris Reynolds is the kind of guy who didn't accept having to choose between passion and profit. He was already miles ahead of the pack because he knew what kind of difference he wanted to make in the world. He never for a moment sat around waiting for circumstances to line up just right so he could get into the action. He had already organized his first charitable trips to help the needy years before he had a proper business model or even a brand.

It was when we started working together that the seeds he had planted, all the little bits and pieces he had already put out into the world, started to come together to form a meaningful picture for the future. Sometimes it's really as simple as learning to look at what you've already done from a new point of view. A good story is more than the ingredients that go into it—it's putting it all together in just the right way so that your audience is instantly engaged.

Now Chris has not only been busy creating trips in destinations like India, Ghana, and Peru to help out the needy, but he has also applied his passion for mutual benefit toward a project called The Entrepreneur House, where like-minded nomadic entrepreneurs live together for months at a time on a different kind of journey. He has transitioned from doing good when he could to being a fully empowered profitable entrepreneur with a clear vision of the future.

As you read Chris' story, try to think of how his situation might apply to your own business (whether you are involved in a similar non-profit or just a passion project). Ask yourself the following questions for maximum impact.

- Why do you believe your project has to remain non-profit? Would transitioning to a profit model adulterate your mission—or possibly enhance it?
- What is the greatest value you provide your customers and contributors beyond the intangible satisfaction of contributing to a good cause? Is there a more visceral and specific way you can productize your mission?
- How many of your hobbies and passion projects have you been delaying turning into real, scalable ventures? What's holding you back from acting on them?

READ CHRIS REYNOLDS' STORY

'My name is Chris Reynolds. I run a website called The One Effect—'One thing can change it all.' I am a digital nomad, world traveller, entrepreneur, and just a person that's out there helping others.

Back in 2009, I read the book *The Four Hour Work Week* by Tim Ferris. I had started a couple of businesses before. The main business I had lasted a couple of years, and it went under due to the recession in 2008 and 2009. It was right around that time that I came across Tim Ferris' book. It presented the idea to me to go out and create some type of money or some type of business earning money online, where you can travel the world and basically gain a sort of liberty—where you can live anywhere you want to, and make money and live out the life of your dreams.

I started building websites, put AdSense on websites, and backlinked them, and I started making a bit of money from that. By 2011, I was ready to move abroad and bought a one-way ticket to Costa Rica.

I had many websites where I would write article after article, and backlink them and put Google AdSense on the site to earn money for marketing. Those were doing alright until April 2011, when Google wrote a new algorithm and completely wiped out the income from those websites. I knew I needed to do something else, and I found some type of work contracting online. Around this time, after being in Costa Rica for a while, I decided to start the idea of what I call, The One Effect.'

FROM HUMBLE CHARITABLE BEGINNINGS

'The One Effect started out as a group of friends deciding to raise some money for a charity, and we had so much fun we decided we wanted to blog about it. I moved to Peru, and we decided we wanted to build a farm for malnourished children as our first project. We ended up building a farm, and after that I moved to Spain and grew the website a little bit more.

The tagline for the website at the time originally was, "Experiments that change the world," because the idea was that a person could take one idea or one dream and go out and really truly make a difference in the world with it. The first year wasn't serious with the website. The second year was more serious. It was a passion project, but it wasn't a fully legitimate business, and that's what I always wanted to move it into, and I didn't really know how.

I didn't know where I wanted to go with it. I knew I wanted to make it into a business that could sustain my lifestyle and could grow and help people at the same time. I always struggled with how I could funnel that so I could have my focus primarily on generating revenue, helping people, and creating a sustainable income.

For a long time, I really felt stuck with where I wanted to go, and I think it was just a fear of making a decision in which direction to go and what market to hit. By working through those really important and often difficult questions and realizing that if I didn't make a decision on it and act on one direction, that I would never make progress.

We talked about experiments to change the world, but nobody really knew what that meant, and that's because I didn't really know where I was going with the business. It wasn't until I was asked the really hard questions when it comes to business and what you're doing with your business, that we started to get some real direction. What kind of narrative do you have with your business? What's your story? Who are you trying to tell it to?

I got a thoroughly harsh critique on my business from Gregory and the direction that I wanted to go with The One Effect. I got a clear vision of what I wanted to do. I revamped the website, rebranded it, and turned it into what I always originally knew that I wanted to do, instead of what I thought I should do. With the new clarity, I put it into a focus where I could make this a fully sustainable business that could keep going on and on and on for years to come.'

TURNING A HOBBY INTO A SUSTAINABLE MISSION

'I think the most important thing I have now is really an idea of what I wanted to grow this into as opposed to just something I did for fun. I turned my hobby into a movement. After we rebranded and reworked the entire design of the website, The One Effect finally has subscribers. We have consistent podcasts. We have consistent blogs of personal development and inspirational content that helps people with their goals and their dreams and their aspirations, while at the same time generating income.

I would say this is a problem that a lot of non-profit or sort of "passion-based" companies and businesses have. They believe strongly in what they're doing, but they don't really know how to propel it forward or to bring in any money to support it. In fact, the problem with a non-profit is just in the name right there: "non-profit." They don't make money, and if something doesn't make money, it can't be sustainable. There is a lot of well-meaning people out there that have great ideas to make a difference in the world, but they'll rob themselves of their own money, or not know how to create a sustainable charity or a business that is for profit.

A lot of people get lost in between one and the other, assuming that you can either have a non-profit and do charity work, or you can have a business. The thing is, we have coming to a time where we can have both. We can have a business that truly helps people, a business that's absolutely sustainable, a business that's focused on both profit and helping people at the same time to put real value into the world and make a difference.

I'm very passionate about creating a better world and helping others go after their dreams and their goals and creating the life of their dreams. The thing is that if we believe in ourselves, we truly have a limitless life. There's nothing that can hold us back to anything we want to do, and traditional education doesn't necessarily teach us that. It teaches us to go out and get a good job and work hard and make money more or less, have a family, retire, and die.

That's the model of the rat race that people go around

over and over and over. A lot of people just don't know that there are other ways to live, that it's completely acceptable and often very times irresponsible not to live a life going after your dreams, not to live a life going after the things that you truly desire in this world.

Ever since I can remember, I pictured myself as an old man, being 95 years old laying on my deathbed and visualizing the type of life that I want to live. So, when I think about that type of life that I want to live as an old man, I think about being a type of person that goes around the world making a difference. I think about being an entrepreneur. I think about growing personally, helping other people grow, inspiring, and really just living the life of my dreams.'

MAKING CHANGE PROFITABLE

'The thing is these trips are just as valuable for the people who pay to go on them as the people they are designed to help. Because one, they get to experience an adventure of a lifetime. Two, they get to get out of their box and grow as a person when they end up in a village building a home for slave children. Three, they get to help people they never thought they would ever meet and also people that they will never ever meet again...and they get to help leave a legacy for changing the world.

There are plenty of inspirational figures out there saying, "Hey, go live the life of your dreams and be amazing." There are plenty of people saying, "Please, help these slave children, because they're slaves, and they're children, and we don't want them to be slave children. Give them some money or volunteer and dig them a well or something." We're about combining these powerful ideas together into one really awesome concept that brings adventure into the mix.

In fact, there's a new kind of phrase calling this adventure charity travel, where people can leave their nine-to-five routine, take two weeks off work, go to Costa Rica, go to Peru, go to Ghana, and really experience life with the natives there, while at the same time helping them create whatever they're trying to create in their lives and have a new adventure of a lifetime. We're creating charity that doesn't have to be self-sacrifice.

What I had noticed with a lot of charity that I had done in the past is that it always misses something. A lot of people do charity because they feel they should do it, and not because they really want to do it, and so they'll sign up for different charity projects or activities where they think they should get some type of fulfillment out of it, but they don't because it's out of guilt really instead of out of passion. When you can blend adventure travel with some type of charity work that people can get really behind and get excited about, then it's a win/win.

Now my long-term vision of The One Effect is to have multiple communities all over the world. We already have three, but to have multiple communities all over the world where we go in and over a long-term basis truly make a difference in those communities is the mission.

Nearly two-and-a-half years ago, we built a farm for malnourished children in Peru, and we actually went and broke ground with the natives on the side of a mountain building this farm. Six months after the project, we started getting pictures about the progress of the farm. Now it's been over two years and the farm is massive. Not only is it feeding children in a village of 60, but it's also feeding families that live in the village.

They get to be tenants to part of the land, and 50 per cent of what they grow goes to the school, and the other 50 per cent goes to their own families.

So, we're actually feeding people on a fully sustainable project because that farm will last for generations. The idea behind that long-term with The One Effect is to have these projects going long-term in India, in Thailand, in Nepal, and Peru, and Costa Rica, all over the world, and making a difference in all these communities while taking people there to experience the culture and help people.

We're going to build up a podcast, continue to blog and inspire people. At the heart of it, The One Effect is an inspirational personal development blog where people can really learn about themselves and grow, and also come along on these adventures and have the time of their lives.'

Case Study #4

Skyrocketing a Personal Brand through Narrative Focus

FEATURING NIEDRA GABRIEL OF SPIRIT MOVES

Niedra Gabriel is a movement coach who specializes in helping people with limited range of motion, to restore their bodies to a state of peak flexibility and performance through bespoke, low-intensity exercises that release years of accumulated stiffness and tension. Her work is now centred around highly specialized motion therapy she does with athletes, recovering injury patients, and aging clientele through international workshops and private classes. You can find her at:

www.spirit-moves.com

INTRODUCTION TO NIEDRA

Sometimes, knowing too much about your business can be more of an obstacle to growth than not knowing enough. It's very easy to get too close to your business and forget how it looks through the eyes of a complete stranger. When I first met Niedra, she had already been practicing her particular craft of motion therapy and training for most of her life. Already in her 60s, she had more skill and experience in her niche than most people will ever get.

Despite the years she had invested into learning about the human body in relation to motion and flexibility, Niedra had neglected something very important. She never learned how to tell the story of what she did in a way that instantly conveyed her compelling uniqueness.

The truth is, the further you develop yourself as a solo professional and service provider, the easier it is to become so obscure that mainstream audiences have trouble understanding you at all. This hurts everyone. Your business stagnates because no one can see what makes your practice appealing, or the explanation they hear is so different from the larger category in their mind that they are already accustomed to. Then the people who need your help the most overlook you completely, and they never experience the potentially powerful benefit of working with you.

In Niedra's case, she had three decades of precedent describing herself as a conventional Yoga and Pilates instructor to work against. The community of dedicated clients she had organically built through word of mouth all loved her, and they were enough to sustain her financially. However, without a strong and unique message, she had no real way to scale her efforts and start putting her brand in front of thousands of viable clients.

By working together closely over the course of several weeks, we were able to probe deeply into Niedra's mind and bring out the gems of information she had stored away inside her vast knowledge on the subject of motion therapy. We homed in on not only the specific benefit she was most qualified to deliver but also the exact people most likely to want it, as well as how she could most effectively package it all together as one emotional brand identity.

Since undergoing this process and implementing the necessary narrative changes into her live events and promotional material, Niedra has finally been able to achieve her lifelong dream of being truly independent in her business. Not only is she making up to 700 per cent more for her time than she did before, but she is now working more often and is in complete control of how, when, and where she runs her workshops. Her audience is growing rapidly with each passing day beyond the initial small community of followers she had cultivated, and she has more opportunities than ever before to practice her craft online and in other new ways.

If you're a skilled solo practitioner of any kind, I want you to think about the obstacles currently stopping you from scaling your business. Just because you operate as an individual, it doesn't mean you can't tell your story in a big way and apply your skills in highly leveraged outlets. The first step to going from one-to-one to one-to-many is having a story worth telling to a much larger and more discerning audience.

And if you find yourself in a similar position to where Niedra was when we started, take the time to reflect on the following questions about your own business. Don't stop inquiring until real, compelling answers become apparent to you. They will give you the insight you need to make lasting changes to your brand identity.

- What do you do that is uniquely valuable compared to other providers in the same genre as yourself?
- Do you use too many generic terms? Do people have a hard time understanding the details of your business?
- Do you know what types of people need your help the most? What can you do to reach out to them and make them realize you are offering a valuable solution to their problems?
- In what ways are you letting externalities limit your brand identity? Are you ever afraid to tell the whole story?

READ NIEDRA GABRIEL'S STORY

'My first introduction to movement was as an aspiring dancer with a lot of technical, physical problems, and with a high level of ambition to become a ballet dancer. That ambition did not succeed. I did not achieve it because I had too many injuries and challenges technically, which is what brought me into the world of movement therapy to restore alignment in the body.

I studied yoga and Pilates in the interim. Going through this work with other people was incredibly fulfilling and fascinating, as I learned that each person has a unique blueprint of how they're put together, and how they move, and how they understand movement, and where it comes from.

I now work with motion and fitness to free up what is blocking people from achieving optimal health. Over the years, I studied many different modalities in order to solve problems like why shoulders are stiff or why the spinal column and the nervous system can be blocked. It's about integrating all this together in order to really elevate the whole standard of living of the person, such as their sense of well-being and their emotional state, so they can have more confidence in who they are and how they operate.

Over the years, I started working with a variety of different clientele, such as aging people who are finding that they're just less comfortable in their body than they used to be. Another group is athletes who are past their peak of performance or who have had an injury and are not sure how to go back into the game safely or regain what they had before and leapfrog to the next level.

The problem for most people is that if they have a certain type of movement they do regularly, like sitting in a chair at the computer all day, or if they're a runner, using their legs within a certain range of motion, or if you're a tennis player it's swinging their right arm and rotating their trunk a certain way, the body kind of freezes up into these shapes without us being aware of it. It hardens into it, and there is a need to start to soften up these hardened areas and restore them to the pristine way they hang in space on the skeleton.

Very few people address that aspect of movement, so there's a pre-ironing out of all the things that are blocking the range of movement and then correctly integrating movement again in a way that allows people to achieve more of their maximum capacity. I work with these people to restore their range of movement, achieve potential, and integrate specific movement on a daily basis into their daily lives so that they are feeling high levels of vitality and energy.

In the Pilates world, I do teacher trainings so other teachers can use that series of movements and techniques and machinery, but very much for my own perspective. I do workshops in both yoga and Pilates specializing on how to release painful tight feet, tight hamstrings, tight shoulders, tight spine, and how to release the tension in your neck and face. These are all generic subjects that are applicable to both students and teachers."

NIEDRA'S FAILURE TO COMMUNICATE AMAZING VALUE

'During my entire three-decade career, I have struggled to articulate what I did for people. I have at various times worked with coaches to progress my business and elevate it and expand, but I never got exactly what I needed. I have always been aware that I have a service that is very desired. But even though I've been told to brand myself, define my specific niche, and describe myself in a way that doesn't make me a commodity on a shelf, I was not able to get down to the nitty-gritty of what I did.

When people asked me what I did, I would say, "I teach yoga or Pilates." One coach forbade me to use those two terms, and I'd ramble around trying to explain what I did. People would look at me with this glazed look in their eyes like, "Huh?" and then somebody would say, "she teaches Pilates and yoga," and everybody would go, "Oh, okay I get it now." So yes, I've had a hard time defining what I do, and hence the range of people that I would contact was limited to people who already knew me and my reputation through word of mouth from friends.

The problem with just calling myself a yoga teacher was that there are many teachers teaching yoga and Pilates, and each teacher and each of the services I offer has a uniqueness to it. Ultimately, that's where it's extremely limiting to say just I teach Pilates. Anybody hearing that may already have a preconceived picture of what that means. So, there's a very, very, very small percentage of people that will become interested in what I do, and that's only if they already have a passion for yoga or Pilates. They like it and they want it.

If they don't know what it is, or they have no interest in going into class when they have a picture in their head of tying yourself up like a pretzel, then they don't even have an interest in talking further to me. Likewise, nor do I have any common ground to open up a conversation with them, because it's not linking the bridge to who they are.

It's kind of like taking a badly tuned piano. First, you must tune each string to the right note, then a master pianist can make music with it. If it's not in tune, it's going to sound lousy no matter who is playing. I make the instrument sound really good. Then it's easy to play good music. The music here is up to the client: running, tennis, dancing, winning the Olympics, gymnastics, yoga, Pilates, having a nice pleasant life, gardening, or whatever they want. It's individualized to the person, so I've learned that defining it in a way that is relatable to their specific interests is extremely important if I want to make an impact.

Within the industry, I'm already defining myself far more specifically. If a yoga teacher wants to increase her knowledge and teaching repertoire, why should she go study from another yoga teacher? There's a hundred to choose from. The moment I define that I am doing a workshop on problem-solving and stepping slightly outside of just the traditional mode, I can attract a lot more professional people who are aware that there is a problem.

Understanding what my program and my service has given me are far more confidence boasting fundamentally to develop new training programs and various services that are specifically geared towards a combination of unravelling problems and then educating the person. I would like to eventually have some kind of a retreat centre where people can embody a lot of these teachings intensively and then leave and go back to their lives with a bunch of tools that they can easily apply at home to keep themselves with increased functionality and diminished pain.'

HOW A CLEARER IDENTITY CREATED A NEW BUSINESS MODEL

'In the interim, I'm already doing retreats of this nature. I also want to develop quite a few online education videos because much of this can be taught via the internet, especially for teacher trainings. The sky really is the limit. At some point, I will also do a 30-day transformation training online, so I can run it from a computer anywhere in the world to a group of people that have signed up.

Although I still consider myself a baby with my understanding of promotion and marketing, I know I will keep growing and learning. I have tools now to reach a much, much larger audience than I ever had before, which has made it all the more important that I really know what to say to them to grab their attention and intrigue them. The momentum of what I can deliver and what I can develop will only accelerate. I have no doubt about it. My website is undergoing a major redesign, so it can represent what I do much better. Up till now, it had been only a newsletter.

My whole business model has changed. I've been going over to Europe for the last five years for retreats, and one of the little events that I was doing there was being a guest presenter at a hotel in Austria. I had a devoted group of followers, who would come, and I would teach a yoga class in the morning and Pilates class in the afternoon, and we'd all hang out together.

It was a small event where I would get a small commission. For me it was a very dissatisfying service because I never felt I was really stepping into what I wanted to do.

So, I decided to re-approach the whole thing. I terminated that contract and found a location in Spain I could work out of and decided to go independent with the help I got, redefining myself and my services from Gregory.

I expanded my old program by up to four-and-a-half hours per day with much more specific agendas as to what's going to be covered physically and emotionally. For me, it was the first time I sent out a newsletter that I was frankly very excited about, because I felt it was raising the bar and it was exactly the kind of bar I wanted to raise for my own quality of service. It has been a dream of mine to do this kind of service, to run this kind of a program and now I'm finally doing it.

That first retreat was a week long. Once I sent my newsletter out to my own mailing lists, it sold out within a week. The intensity and speed with which people emailed back blew me away. I had never had that kind of response before, and I didn't even have a shopping cart where people could sign up. I had to send everybody a PayPal invoice one at a time. It kind of shocked me, so I went and checked and reserved the same location for the prior week, then sent out two or three more mailings. That week is now full as well. I'm actually still pondering if I want to open up even another week.

So now instead of one possible week of retreats, I've got two full ones and possibly a third one because there's a trickle of people that want to come and have not been able to. So, this is a game changer for me. Numbers-wise, I'm going from making between two and three thousand dollars, to making a profit of probably ten thousand, fifteen thousand, seventeen thousand in that week. I also have some products I'm planning to sell for the first time ever, which will be part of the program. So, I definitely anticipate increasing that.

I have a whole bunch of people who contacted me from Europe who could not make the Spain retreat. I'll have a weekend of workshops taking place, and they are already looking forward to that. So, I anticipate selling out for those two weekends as well and probably getting quite a few private clients. Just by articulating where my passion lies, what I'm interested in, and how I see the nature of the problems that people have, that's opened the door for many new people to approach and contact me.

In the past, sometimes I wondered if I was going to be in the red because it was a bit of a gamble for me to do these. I had to buy my own plane ticket. Sometimes I had to take care of most of my own accommodations. I was just stepping out on a limb because I felt it's the right thing to do. This time I have no doubt that I'm definitely in the black, and probably most of the money will be in before I start, and then I have workshops that will bring a separate amount in. It's a big game changer, and this is just the beginning.

I've had a lot of people contact me saying, "Oh my God. I got your newsletter from my friend, and can I come too?" So, people were forwarding my newsletter about the retreat because of the compelling verbiage. I shouldn't say it went viral because that's such a big scale, but it was being passed on, because obviously I was addressing pain points that other people have and is a concern for them. So, I was providing. I was describing a problem and a solution in a way that I've never done before, and it's made a huge difference.

This is all a result of understanding a little bit better how to articulate, and also find out what they're thinking about, and what my suggestions are, and how to build material to deliver that'll provide service for them, and really resolve what they would like to address in their education.'

WHERE PAST COACHES FAILED

'As I said, I have worked with other coaches, more as group lessons. I have spent a lot of money that I really didn't have, thousands and thousands of dollars with coaches that were master marketers and want to push every button and promise you the sky and the moon as a result of their services. I attended their training programs which were done online—a lot of webinars. I never got results. A lot, I tried to apply. Some, I just gave up because it felt so foreign to me.

So anyhow, I decided I was not going to work with coaches for a while because I was getting no benefit. I seemed to do better on my own and stay calmer and have less of my weak spots irritated with the button pushing to get me to give them more money. When I met Gregory, I knew I would like to work with someone again, but I definitely wanted to work one-on-one. Frankly, it had to be within a budget that was realistic to who I am and what I make, rather than hocking my last dollar because someone is promising me some universe that will never be.

What was different this time was the amount of care that was taken not just with the structure of what I need to do, but actually working with me to walk me through the steps to define and discover who I am and what I do.

It was a very interesting experience, because I would be asked about what I do. I would say, "I teach yoga." "Why should

I care? What do you do in yoga class? What do you do in Pilates?" "I've been teaching for 30 years." I would be bumbling around, stumbling, and stuttering and feeling like this complete idiot using words I knew were not going to express much of anything, because I really couldn't define it easily, or find what I do, or how do I do it.

I call this process "being walked through the stupidity swamp," because obviously something good was being defined. I do have a service, but I couldn't find the words, and having the time to work through that was priceless.

That's what the other coaches didn't do. They tell you to do this and this and this, and then they leave. They take your money and then they go, and then you're left with your inability to apply and a lot of self-criticism that maybe the problem is that you're just lazy or not persistent. The previous coaches never cared whether the client got to the other side. They just delivered the goods and walked away. However, this time, I got the exact transcripts and recordings of what we had gone through with each one of the sessions so I could re-listen to them, see them, and pick out the little gems of gold that were buried in all of the confusion, so I could extract them and make my own.'

LOOKING TO THE FUTURE

'Now I've got someone great managing the website, because my expertise is developing a product, delivering a service, and working live with people. My dream has always been to be able to focus there and really have the majority of the marketing and online aspects taken over by someone else, but it has to be my thing. It has to represent who I am. I know no successful person does it alone. You do need a team. You do need people to work with, and they need to be geniuses in their own field, and so I am very much looking forward to continuing my business development.

I have never been more excited about what the future of my business holds.'

Case Study #5

Embracing Personality in a Technical Niche

FEATURING OLIVIER WAGNER OF 1040 ABROAD

Olivier Wagner is a tax preparer and offshore consultant who specializes in Americans who live, work and invest overseas. His unique background of immigrating to the US and running a business while travelling the world has enabled him to focus his profession on the areas of the US tax code that changes the rules for uncommon lifestyles and sources of income. He also helps individuals gain greater freedom through citizenship renunciation, offshore banking/incorporation, and other little-known strategies to legally minimize tax obligation. You can find out more about Olivier's work at: www.1040abroad.com.

INTRODUCTION TO OLIVIER

Olivier has one of the most interesting personal backgrounds of anyone I've ever worked with, and one of our primary goals of working together was to figure out the best way to use his personal brand to his advantage in a convoluted industry.

The moment people start thinking about taxes, they tense up emotionally. They are legally obligated to pay, and their greatest concern becomes about minimizing their burden as much as possible and making sure they are reporting accurately so they can avoid the potentially huge consequences of failing to do so. These become even greater concerns for people who earn their income or spend a lot of time overseas, as the tax rules are much more complicated, and it's very easy to make a mistake if you aren't deeply familiar with the system in place.

This is what Olivier had to help his clients realize, and he had to learn to use his personality and image to make that easier for them, which he was a bit reluctant to do at first. His focus had always been on the hard and fast rules of the internal revenue code, something he had soaked up into his mind like an information sponge. While this made him incredibly qualified to help his target market of Americans based internationally, it blinded him toward how to best earn their trust and deliver his vitally important message of saving them money and keeping them out of jail through superior tax compliance.

Working with Olivier, I helped him to see that impressive as his technical understanding of tax strategies were, he was going to need something more to stand out from other competitors who made similar claims. He was going to have to attract people to him with his personal story and way of engaging the people he worked with, and that meant he had to become the face of his own company. His technical prowess would then serve to validate the initial feelings new prospects felt when they intuitively decided Olivier was the kind of person they wanted to help them with their tax goals.

Olivier now has a completely new website and overall branding position to be promoting himself from, which in turn has allowed him to double the amount he was previously charging to prepare tax returns. He has expanded his services to include bespoke offerings, which have significantly increased the total lifetime customer value of the people he works with.

Shortly after overhauling his online presence, my publishing company, Identity Publications, also worked with Olivier to write and publish his first book, *U.S. Taxes for Worldly Americans: The Traveling Expat's Guide to Living, Working, and Staying Tax Compliant Abroad*. It was a targeted brand-building effort designed to set him apart from other accountants in his industry through an impressive display of knowledge and unique personality. Since Olivier's book is the only one on Amazon to cover the complex subject of American international taxation adequately, it quickly became a bestseller in multiple Amazon categories. In addition to earning ongoing passive income from book royalties, *U.S. Taxes for Worldly Americans* continues to generate a healthy stream of new clientele from the readers who digest his comprehensive message and trust his authority on the sensitive subject of overseas tax and income. Books are just another tool in a wide arsenal for entrepreneurs with a message worth studying.

As you read Olivier's story, look at his progress through the lens of your own business struggles. Even if you don't want to ever become a personality brand with your name and face plastered everywhere, you can still take measures to create a personality for your business itself.

- Have you been putting too much focus on the technical

value of what you offer, neglecting the human element? What steps can you take to add personality without diminishing expertise?

- Have you done enough to make your audience realize how your specialization differentiates you from generic providers in the same industry? What are you doing to get in front of and educate the exact right people who need your specialization?
- Do your website and other marketing materials tell too much? Are you overwhelming your audience with information, instead of gently inviting them to get more involved?

READ OLIVIER WAGNER'S STORY

'I prepare US tax returns for US citizens outside the US through my company, 1040 Abroad. I grew up in France, close to Strasbourg, and I always wanted to leave. When I came to the US, I first studied in Louisiana for a year, and then I worked in finance in New York. I married a US citizen. I got my US green card. I got my US citizenship, and in 2011 we moved to Canada. So, the French government sees me as being French, but I see myself as being American, even though I still have this international background. I'm not American in the way that other people are because I didn't grow up there, but I did legally immigrate.

I feel like I have a unique, blended experience of being both a foreigner and an American, and now an American expatriate. I've seen all sides of the spectrum, and this has really shaped how I present myself to the people I work with. It's important because I work with three very distinct types of clients living outside the US who need help:

1. Digital nomads
2. Expatriates
3. Accidental Americans

A digital nomad is basically the same as the term "PT" or "perpetual traveller." It's somebody who travels all the time, and as such does not have enough ties to any given country to become a taxpayer. They travel on tourist visas or at most student visas, and they probably have businesses online. It's great to earn money online when you're not a US citizen because you don't have to pay taxes anywhere. You don't have to file a return anywhere. Yet, if you are a US citizen then you still have to file a tax return anyway. So, my job is to help them figure out how to allocate the tax time and minimize what they have to pay legally.

Most people know about the Foreign Earned Income Exclusion, which allows them to exclude up to about a hundred thousand dollars of foreign income. There's also a physical presence test, which means spending at least 330 days in any 12-month period outside the US.

When I talk about expatriates, however, I mean Americans who live outside the US with a more stable lifestyle in another country. They might have moved to Switzerland to work for a large bank but are still American. Maybe they finished studying at university and they got this great job in Switzerland. So, they move there. They open their regular Swiss bank account to receive their pay cheque, and sooner or later they end up marrying a Swiss person and having a child over there.

Expats pay taxes in the foreign country where they live, which allows them to use a foreign tax credit. They already pay tax in a foreign country, and they're more likely not to have to pay tax at all in the US.

An accidental American is somebody who does not consider themselves to be American. They typically were born in the US, which is why they are an American citizen, but moved overseas at a young age. A lot of times, they might not even know that they are American. They are unaware of any consequences they might have. This is a major risk that a lot of people are subject to. Most people have never heard the term "accidental American," and they don't know that you could be American and not know it.

Starting last year, there's a new law that is implemented by foreign banks. It's called FATCA, and it means banks now identify which of their clients are Americans, and forward that person's name, address, and account balance to the IRS. Furthermore, anyone who has a balance of more than ten thousand dollars in a foreign bank account at any point during the year has to file an FBAR report. So, when the IRS receives this data, they will try to match that to the taxpayer on record, and the penalty for wilfully failing to file an FBAR could be up to 50 per cent of the account balance per year.'

THE IMPORTANCE OF SPECIALIZATION IN A DYNAMIC INDUSTRY

'A regular US tax preparer is only familiar with the tax laws that apply to his country. So, if you're coming from New Orleans, Louisiana, and you had your tax preparer prepare your tax returns for the past five years, and all of a sudden you decide to become a digital nomad and open foreign bank accounts and set up foreign corporation, it means there are going to be rules your previous tax guy is not familiar with. You will be his first ever client who will be in this kind of situation and is going to have to learn the knowledge to help you file correctly and minimize your tax obligation. He might not even be aware that some forms need to be filled out.

More and more people are renouncing their US citizenship now than ever before to avoid all the complicated tax burdens that come with the territory. An additional part of my job is to educate them about the possibility of processes like this for themselves and complete their renunciation if that's what is best for them. A lot of people don't even know how easy it is to get rid of your American citizenship.

Another thing is just getting tax compliant, because a lot of people have never filed taxes or haven't filed in a very long time. It's a very important subject with potentially very large consequences. Still, so many people don't pay any attention to it at all, because it is all so overwhelming for the average person. To some people, it's actually offensive even to address the whole concept of taxes.'

BECOMING A REAL BUSINESS

'Before, my business wasn't really a business at all. I worked for a large accounting firm, and I had started a blog on my own as an offshore tax expert. I managed to attract an attorney who was doing renunciation of US citizenship, and I've been partnering with him since to get most of my clientele. I wrote a very technical blog that older tax professionals liked, and which showed I was a tax professional who knows his stuff, but when regular people would go there they just got put to sleep by how dull and complicated all the information was.

I had bought my website from a company which specializes in accountants' websites, but the trouble is that they seemed to work for the kind of accountants for whom the website is only a business card, more or less. I knew I needed more if I was going to convince strangers that I was the tax specialist they could trust with such a difficult and important subject. I've tried to find solutions for this before.

Finally, I knew it was time to get serious and create a new web presence to call my own, as well as create a marketing strategy and stronger brand identity to get people to come to me. We worked to create my website to generate leads, to capture people's emails, to contact them, follow up, offer PDF downloads, and things like that, which was something that I always wanted to do before. I just did not know how to piece everything together. I've read article after article about marketing, but I just was not able to put it into play. I know a lot of things, but I didn't know how to use it, and that froze me up for a long time.'

COMMUNICATING MORE CLEARLY AND EXPANDING SERVICES

'I really had two major problems. First, my message was much too complicated. It wasn't speaking to my actual audience, even though I knew who they were and what they needed. I was talking in a way that had very little impact on them. Second, I didn't know how to use the right tools to get that message out, which is what I'm doing now that I have a much cleaner, easier-to-understand message. To me, it goes beyond just the actual words I'm saying in person or on my website. It's about the personality I can show off and stand out in my industry with.

The future for me is now about getting more work to

generate more income. The dream is to be able to outsource it with other accountants and be able to create almost completely passive income, but for now, I want to be busy getting my message out there.

I also want to expand my services and expand the value I provide beyond just filing tax returns. I'm looking into the area of incorporation. I'm looking into returns for non-residents, and then I can provide entries for green cards. There's a lot of advice on I can offer on living as an expat. Everything from mailbox services in the US, where you can still have your mail sent locally, and more. I've been an expat, in a way, since 2004, but I've been a US expat since 2011.

Ultimately, I'm in a position to service many aspects of helping people be better expatriates, better digital nomads, and live internationally beyond just the tax side of things. Once I've helped them with that, there are a lot of other needs I could help fulfil for them. I've been banking outside the US. I've been receiving mail outside the US. I've been maintaining a driving license. I can even give suggestions on how to get immigration status in another country. This has been an important part of the expansion of my brand identity.

A lot of people are working in an industry where they're held back by the specific, highly technical nature of what they're doing. They're having a really hard time making a name for themselves because the niche they're in is so complicated and they don't know how to communicate how important what they're doing is or why somebody should want to work with them.

My advice is that you need to find somebody who understands that. Just like for me, people don't understand offshore taxation as an American citizen, so they come to me. I don't understand brand identity this way, so I turn to the people who can help me figure this out and prepare my messaging platform for me. Don't be scared of trying new things or growing in new directions, because that's how you get results you couldn't have with what you were doing before.'

SECTION V

RESOURCES FOR PROSPECTIVE ENTREPRENEURS

Introduction to Resources for Prospective Entrepreneurs

The eternal question of how to make money has haunted mankind for as long as money has existed as a medium of exchange. Those who don't have it, want it. Those who have it, want more of it. The fundamental failing of the unsuccessful is to accept that money flows from one life to another through fate or uncontrollable circumstances. It's not terribly difficult to understand how and why money changes hands and taking the time to solidify this foundation in your mind will aid you in any business you start or professional heights you climb.

Maybe you're not at the point where you have a small business to support your lifestyle. Maybe you don't even have your first big entrepreneurial idea for a revolutionary product or service. It's common for the initial motivation for running your own business to be nothing more than the desire to leave your conventional work life behind and make money on your own terms. Or maybe you are very young like I was and have no real career path to abandon at all, but you know you want to be in control of your own life.

There are tons of resources already on the web for

people who have learned how to build an online business or independent company. However, their advice usually pertains to more technical matters of management that only make sense to someone already running a functioning business. The guy sitting in his cubicle with aspirations of breaking out doesn't need to know how to double his Facebook fans. He needs to learn the axioms of making money on his own.

In fact, business newbies are likely to get discouraged if they are only exposed to advice far beyond their present understanding. There were many times during my patchwork self-education that I was left wondering, 'Ok. So now what do I do with that information?' after reading a lengthy blog post or listening to a podcast by an established 'expert.' The information gap between the people who are doing it and those who want to do it is simply too large.

THE AXIOMS OF MAKING MONEY

Whether you are 16 or 60, you will need these as the foundation of your actions, if you want to succeed with any business idea. There are only three ways a person can acquire more money:

1. Steal it
2. Beg for it
3. Earn it

These are easy enough to understand. Stealing is when you take money without the permission of its owner. This can be as simple as back alley pickpocketing, or as elaborate as the creation of fake companies backed by fake promises to deliver large amounts of value but never fulfilling them. I've had lots of experience as the victim of both varieties of theft.

Begging for money is a bit more innocent, but hardly more admirable than stealing. Begging is when we attempt to appeal to the sympathies of others and get them to give us their money without offering anything in return. Their only reward is a fleeting sense of self-righteousness or the alleviation of guilt. While the transfer may be voluntary, there is no sustainable, scalable, or repeatable value exchange occurring. Non-profits and charities need to be cautious of falling into a position of begging for generic donations.

Earning money happens when something of greater subjective value is offered in exchange for the amount of money being received. The value is offered as products and services—or things and actions which deliver a specific result. This is obviously what we want to focus on as entrepreneurs and as philanthropic human beings in general. Measurable progress can only be made when focus is taken away from stealing or begging for money, and instead put into earning it.

APPLYING STRUCTURE TO AN IDEA

In its most basic form, earning a living means trading an hour of your life to your employer for a fixed wage. However, unless you become a doctor or a lawyer, there are strict monetary limits on this simplistic time-for-money profit model. Structure enables you to take a valuable concept and exponentially magnify its influence and earning potential. This structure allows you to leverage your time, and therefore earn higher and higher amounts of money for the same level of input. You can even set up a structure that runs mostly or entirely independently of you, earning ongoing passive income.

You don't need a formal business plan to get started making

money independently or add structure to a basic and valuable idea. Here's how anyone with a good idea can start making at least a little bit of money on day one of implementation:

1. Create something of value—either a product or a service.
2. Identify the type of person who needs it most.
3. Compare it to similar solutions in regard to function, message and price.
4. Describe it concisely, including what it does, how it works, who it's for and what makes it unique.
5. Figure out how to get this message in front of the people who need it most.
6. Take their money and give them the product or perform service in return.

This is simple in principle but gets more complex the bigger your idea or the more you attempt to scale it. To create a more complex product or service, you will need to identify manufacturers and suppliers who can provide all the different parts you need at a price that is significantly lower than what you can charge for the finished product. These are the kinds of businesses that typically take both time and a fair amount of start-up capital to get going. They may not see a profitable return for months or years and are therefore not as appealing to bootstrapped first-time entrepreneurs.

If you are not in a position to make profits from the very beginning that you can reinvest into the business, you can seek out an infusion of cash from an investor in exchange for some ownership in the company, or an instant royalty on everything sold.

THE ROLE OF AN ENTREPRENEUR

As an entrepreneur, your job is to hold the whole business together, and plan its future. At the start of your first business, you and whoever else is on your team of founders will probably be handling most of the tasks yourself—all the way from production to distribution, to sales and marketing. As you grow, you should begin to rely on technology and other people to handle the tasks which do not require your direct intervention. In time, you will be able to structure your business in a way where you are only left dealing with the tasks you are best qualified to handle. That is when you will start making more and more money for far less work than you would previously have thought possible.

The ideal role of a founder is that of the master strategist at the heart of the company. Yet, most CEOs and other leaders end up taking on the role of gap-filler. They hire specialized employees to take care of the major functions to keep the business running, but little things inevitably pop up that fall on the boss' shoulders to take care of. It's common for founders caught filling the gaps in their company management to run out of the time to implement new strategies and test new ideas. Often, the person who should be taking on the highest-level tasks is relegated to busywork and maintenance instead. It's not emotionally rewarding, and it's potentially lethal to your business.

As the leader in your business, your time is the most valuable asset you have. When you are confident in the value of your own time, you realize how important it is to delegate tasks which can be done to the same level of quality by someone else for a reasonable price. Work to turn your company's daily tasks into processes which can be passed on to others. Simplify what you do every day and identify whatever ways your current employees are already wasting effort and resources. All it takes is a mind attuned to efficiency in all things to turn a functioning business into a scalable profit-producing machine.

REPUTATION, RELATIONSHIPS AND MORALITY

A successful business is defined by relationships, and those relationships are forged because of the reputations of the individuals or entities involved. Your reputation as an individual entrepreneur is the informal start to your official brand identity. Everyone who does not exist in a social vacuum has one. It's the perception other people have of you and the elevated starting position new connections are willing to grant you based on what others have told them about you.

Reputations can either be accurate or completely fabricated. The best ones are forged organically through the real interactions you have with others so that they are free to form their own positive opinion about your character and abilities. This is a far stronger type of positive impression than any you could create by talking yourself up or fooling others into thinking a certain way about you.

Trust comes in two forms, and both are extremely important. The first type of trust relates to your competency. If someone is going to willingly give you the authority to perform a skilled task or advise them in a specialized field of knowledge, they must believe that you know what you are doing. We all do this many times every day. When you board a plane, you are implicitly agreeing that you trust the pilot to get you to your destination safely and that you will not attempt to commandeer the aircraft yourself out of fear that he doesn't know what he's doing.

The most knowledgeable and talented people tend to become well-known in their fields. Malcolm Gladwell dubbed these people as mavens in his book, *The Tipping Point*, and many of them eventually become synonymous with an entire field of knowledge or branch of skilled labour. Michael Jackson was the king of pop. Richard Dawkins is known, somewhat tongue in cheek, as one of the four horsemen of modern atheism (and the acknowledged authority on evolution). David Wolfe is the face of raw food health trends. Do people trust your competency in your chosen field?

The second type of trust has to do with morality. It's about a person's willingness to mislead or harm another through the use of physical force or psychological fraud. Entrepreneurs cannot survive if they surround themselves with people who are likely to steal from them or lie about important information. You cannot forge a meaningful relationship with someone who is willing to take what he wants from you against your will or trick you into doing something against your own best interest.

Just as individuals build a reputation for their competency in a specific domain, they also build one for their moral character. These reputations are built by demonstrating ability and character first-hand and relying on the testimony of others who have personally witnessed it. When someone else publicly vouches for you, they are intertwining their own reputation with yours. Whenever you fail to live up to the standards of the reputation preceding you, you can also bring down everyone who has ever voluntarily associated with you.

The more developed a business or a society as a whole, the more important the role of competence and character reputation becomes. You might be the smartest, most talented, most honest, most generous person on the planet—but if no one who matters knows about it, it won't do you much good in business. Everyone must learn where the line falls between being humble about their own positive attributes, but also not hiding them from the world.

Total morality is the only logical choice for someone who is serious about growing a business and living a meaningful life. An immoral person has the opportunity to improve their life only in the short term. Moral people are incentivized to stay away from them for their own safety. Over a long enough period of time, a natural segregation occurs between those who act honestly and those who intentionally deceive. Those with money have a lot of incentive to not to let any of it fall into the hands of deceitful people. Character analyses and reputation become vital survival skills in this environment.

Ethical people know that there is so much more to be gained by building a reputation as a good person than by being a swindler who will take advantage of others for personal gain. Seek out these righteous people to align yourself with, and they will seek you out as well. If people perceive you can't be trusted with small responsibilities, they won't likely give you large responsibilities.

If you are the type of person who is always telling white lies or showing up late everywhere you go, these seemingly innocuous sins may be responsible for cutting you off from opportunities you never even knew you had. Just because no one ever directly approaches you about your minor indiscretions, doesn't mean they don't notice and remember. The loss of your reputation is the price you pay for the momentary advantages of lazy or immoral behaviour.

I talked in the introduction about a woman I had hired to help me produce the manuscript for this book and market it to bestseller status on Amazon. When she failed to produce the generous results she told me I was paying for, she had every opportunity to make restitution simply by admitting error and refunding my money. I even offered to let her donate the full amount of my purchase to a non-profit education group if she felt more comfortable doing that than refunding the money directly to me. Instead, she chose to cut off all contact with me and disavow any obligation to deliver what she had promised.

I could have taken her to small claims court to recover the $5,000 I paid, and potentially even more because of the huge delays I faced. Instead, I chose to share my extremely negative experience of working with her publicly. Due to the fact that we shared so many mutual connections, she experienced an enormous drop in her professional reputation. I was contacted by many people shortly afterward who thanked me for bringing her immoral behaviour and professional fraud to light so that they knew not to pursue working with her as they had initially planned.

In the long run, she undoubtedly lost a lot more than $5,000 in business because of the short-term gain from ripping me off. That is a stigma which will now follow her around for the rest of her professional life. To have any sustainable success as an entrepreneur, you must protect the reputation of yourself and your brand at all costs.

Don't be afraid to adopt morality as an absolute principle in your life. Be honest with the people you know. Go out of your way to be fair and earnest with others, even if it means a momentary lessening of your own circumstances in life. High-quality individuals notice this behaviour in others and will respond to it appropriately. They will let you into their lives and offer you greater opportunities for collaboration.

When you do mess up and wrong another person, the burden falls squarely upon you to reverse the negative effects of your actions. Most people are willing to forgive a first offense if it is minor and if it is clear that every attempt at restitution is made. Good people generally want to see others evolve into good people too, and they will give you the chance to prove yourself if you appear sincere in your quest to reacquire good moral standing.

Likewise, don't be afraid to appropriately judge the character of others. Read into body language and speaking style. Learn to detect inconsistencies, intentional vagueness, and outright misdirection. Each of these is a red flag for what could become major issues later on, costing you enormous time and money. Monitor how well they communicate with you on simple matters, including the times they omit important information. Observe how they follow through with promises or if they take on too much responsibility.

When you can see all human relationships through this filter, you will be ready to start exchanging and collaborating with others who are in a position to give you what you need to get where you want to go. Nobody does it alone.

APPENDIX 1

Entrepreneurial Terms Defined

If you are not yet an entrepreneur, it might seem like starting your own company is just too complicated. Every new subject appears that way at first. You've probably read a lot of new terms or seen old terms used in unfamiliar ways. There is even some disagreement among professionals exactly what these words mean. Within the context of this book, I'd like to define how they are used.

BRAND IDENTITY

Your brand identity is the collective interpretation your audience maintains for your business. If you are marketing yourself as an expert on a subject, your brand identity is what they think of you as an individual. For most small businesses, it will involve the creation of a name accompanied by a series of visual imagery and verbal messages, which convey a specific personality and function.

CALL TO ACTION

A call to action is the part of any sales process where your audience is prompted to make a decision or do something they otherwise would not have done. It is the whole point of whatever your sales pitch or marketing piece is. You might be trying to generate more subscribers for your email list or closing a sale on a specific product. Whatever it is, you need to be clear about where you are directing your prospects.

CORE VALUES

Core values are the patterns of change that determine a person's actions. They are the ideals which cause the greatest states of happiness and unhappiness. They are also the primary ways in which people formulate their identity. Brand identities are also forged by the core values of the founders of companies. They are reflected in their messaging and create unique engagement for a specific audience.

CROSS-SELLING

Cross-selling is similar to upselling, except that the initial sale is used to pitch other offerings which complement, but do not replace, the original order. If someone buys a shirt from you, it is reasonable to assume they may also need pants and socks. The stronger the theme linking your offerings, the easier they will be to cross-sell, as anyone who finds value in one is likely to find value in others.

ENGAGEMENT

Engagement is what happens when your audience cares enough about what you are saying to listen and act in response to your message. It is the goal of all forms of sales and marketing. Engagement can be created by presenting your brand and its products in an identifiable way—appealing to a core value, or a major source of pain or pleasure.

LEAD

A lead is any prospect who has been qualified and shown a genuine interest in purchasing from you. They are nearly ready to make a purchasing decision, just as soon as they are presented with the information or motivation which will push them to complete the sale. 'Dead,' 'cold,' 'warm,' and 'hot' are all used to describe how close a lead is to completing a purchase.

LIFETIME CUSTOMER VALUE

Lifetime customer value is the sum total of everything the average client will spend with you once they become a customer. It is a useful figure for a long-term perspective on growing your business or for planning the use of minimum viable products, cross-selling, and upselling.

MARKETING

Marketing is the act of making more people aware of the existence of a product, service, or brand. It usually leads directly into sales. Often, the two can be almost indistinguishable as they occur in one swift process.

MINIMUM VIABLE PRODUCT (MVP)

Your minimum viable product is the easiest (and often) smallest complete transfer of value you can offer your audience. It is meant to present the fewest possible obstacles and objections for a newcomer to begin doing business with you. MVPs are usually intended to be upsold or cross-sold into larger purchases later on or used as a way to gather contact information for ongoing marketing.

MORALITY

Moral action is action which does not involve force or trickery. It is any sort of voluntary and informed collaboration among separate parties. In the context of business, it means fulfilling every claim about what your products and services can do and living up to the obligations you set for partnerships with other organizations.

NARRATIVE

Narratives are ways we structure information to make it more meaningful, relatable, and memorable. In business, this means describing your brand, employees, and products as an experience with specific effects for your customer, rather than as a list of static adjectives and features. Your brand narrative is a story, not a compilation of data.

OBJECTIONS

Buying objections are any reasons a prospect may have for not completing a purchase with you. Legitimate objections are those that make them unable to derive the full value of what you are selling (such as lack of funds or lack of need). Illegitimate objections are false excuses and emotional hesitation which halt a beneficial decision.

PRODUCT

A product is a physical method of delivering a specific type of value in a definable and repeatable way. Products can be informational in nature, such as books and videos, or they can be functional tools like hammers, cars, and clothes. Separate products with a similar theme or complementary function can also be grouped together and sold as one collective product, sometimes referred to as a package.

PRODUCTIZED SERVICE

A productized service is what happens when skilled actions are structured in definable and repeatable ways and then presented as fixed goods. They are necessary for service providers to shift from charging for the time they spend performing a service to charging for delivering a specific result. Taking your car in for an oil change usually comes with a fixed cost for the labour and goods involved.

PROOF OF CONCEPT

Proof of concept is anything which demonstrates to your audience that the claims you make are true. It can be as subtle as mentioning real examples of how your product has benefited other people in situations similar to your prospect. It can be as obvious as a live demo of the product itself.

PROSPECT

A prospect is anyone who fits the basic description of your target audience. Until you know more about them and put them through the process of qualification, they should be considered of low importance and not be given too much of your time or money resources. A large prospect database can be filtered into better quality leads, and, eventually, a certain per cent closed on sales to become customers.

QUALIFICATION

Qualification is the process of determining whether or not a prospect has both the problem that your product/service solves and the means to purchase. This process is done for both your sake and the prospect's sake, to save time and ensure satisfaction with the purchase. When a prospect has been qualified and has displayed interest, they are then considered to be a lead and should be approached to close a sale.

SALES

Sales is the act of demonstrating to a qualified lead that a product or service will provide a greater amount of happiness than whatever amount will be lost in the process of using it. A sale is complete when an individual has made the informed decision to exchange their time, money, and whatever else is required for it.

SERVICE

If a product is a noun or a thing, a service is a verb or an action. It is skilled labour performed by an actor to deliver a specific result. It can also be informational or functional—ranging from private piano lessons to automotive repairs. Like products, they can also be packaged together as a collective service with a specific goal.

TARGET AUDIENCE/DEMOGRAPHIC

Your target audience is the group of people who are most likely to find high value in your products and services. The more specifically you have structured your value proposition and brand identity, the more specific your target audience will be. The purpose of having a target audience is so you can focus your communication style, marketing, and sales on the people for whom it will have the greatest effect.

UNIQUE SELLING PROPOSITION (USP)

Your Unique Selling Proposition is whatever distinct value you offer from others in your niche. It can apply to your brand (such as the quality of customer service, price-to-quality ratio, or overall brand personality), or just a specific product (such as solving a specific problem better than any other product). Effective USPs blend many distinct elements into a unique customer experience.

UPSELLING

Upselling occurs when a successful sale has already been made, followed by an additional purchase for something related to the first. An upsell is usually something which would have little value without the initial purchase, such as seat covers for a recently acquired car (i.e. you don't need seat covers if you don't have seats). It improves upon or replaces the initial purchase. It is the antithesis of downselling, which involves something of lesser value.

VALUE OR VALUE PROPOSITION

Value is anything which brings an individual to a higher state of subjective happiness. It is dependent on a person's self-defined goals. The more specifically a product or service can deliver happiness, the more value it will have. A value proposition is a specific claim about the effect your products or services can have on customers. It is the result of using what you sell, not the traits of the object or action.

APPENDIX 2

50 Useful Starting Questions for New Entrepreneurs

QUESTIONS FOR BREAKING OLD HABITS

1. How content are you with your current lifestyle? Do you feel fulfilled or are you seeking something more meaningful or exciting?
2. What are the major pain points you are dealing with in your life right now? How long have they been a factor?
3. Do you feel stifled by the conventional expectations of the people around you?
4. What steps have you taken to overcome these obstacles? How successful have you been?
5. What long-time ambitions have you been putting off because the time never felt 'right'?
6. What social or emotional patterns from your past prevent you from adopting a lifestyle you really want?

QUESTIONS FOR FINDING YOUR ENTREPRENEURIAL INSPIRATION

1. What are the most intrinsic values you hold?
2. What is unique or uncommon about you?
3. What talents, interests, or experiences would you like to build your new business or career around?
4. What are the biggest questions people ask about your passions? What are the biggest problems they need solved?
5. What do you feel are your professional strengths and skills? Weaknesses?
6. What is the most valuable insight or information you can offer the world?
7. How will this new type of work contribute to the lifestyle you actually want? How do you know you won't just end up back in the same place you are now?
8. Do you have any active influences in your life who encourage and support you toward your unconventional lifestyle goals?

QUESTIONS FOR DETERMINING LIFESTYLE LOGISTICS

1. How do you currently sustain yourself financially? Are you happy with the amount of money and the type of work you are doing?
2. If you quit your job tomorrow, how long could you live comfortably without totally depleting your savings?
3. Growing your business is going to require a lot of your time, and possibly money as well. How much time and money can you invest into the development of your business right now?

4. Is this your first time attempting a business? What other relevant experience do you have?

QUESTIONS FOR OPTIMIZING A FLEDGLING BUSINESS

1. What is your goal for your business? Describe its ideal state and your role within it.
2. How much social influence do you personally have? What about your brand?
3. Which is more important to you right now—quick income generation or long-term brand growth?
4. If your business doubled tomorrow, would you be prepared to handle it? Could you fulfil all orders and keep everything running smoothly? What about if it tripled or quadrupled?

QUESTIONS FOR FINDING YOUR COMPANY NARRATIVE

1. Tell me about the intrinsic value of your product(s) (i.e. what practical problem do they solve?).
2. Tell me about the emotional value of your product(s) (i.e. how they make people feel and the values they represent?).
3. What is unique or uncommon about your business compared to others in the same industry?
4. Where did the inspiration for the business come from?
5. Who is the person most likely to want to buy from you? Describe them as well as possible.
6. Is your personal brand as the founder a major part of the appeal of your business? Do you want it to be?
7. What valuable information can you provide your audience about the values your business stands for?
8. What other industries or companies do you know of that

could benefit from your product(s) and narrative? How could you benefit from those of other companies?

QUESTIONS FOR DEVELOPING PRODUCTS AND SERVICES

1. What is the product/package you are promoting as your introductory offer?
2. What other offers do you want to cross-promote or upsell with it?
3. How do these additional offers complement or improve upon the initial offer?
4. What makes your offer unique and irresistible compared to others in the same class?
5. What qualifies a prospect to get enormous value from your offer?
6. List all the possible pain points your offer can solve.
7. How will you reduce or eliminate the buyer's risk from purchasing these products?

QUESTIONS FOR QUALIFYING PROSPECTS

1. What might prevent a person from getting the fullest possible value from your offer?
2. What requirements do they have to meet to actually be able to purchase?
3. What foreseeable objections might someone have to purchasing your products, even if they are qualified?
4. What product or service do most people currently use to fill the role of yours?
5. What is their previous experience purchasing this kind of product?

QUESTIONS FOR FIGURING OUT YOUR COMPANY METRICS

1. How many units are you selling every month?
2. What is the average price per product?
3. What is the average order total?
4. What are your profit margins?
5. How much money do your clients spend on repeat purchases? (lifetime customer value)
6. What products are selling most or least?
7. How do you acquire new clients? How many new prospects per month?
8. How do you keep in touch with existing clients? How often?

APPENDIX 3

Making Money Online

How to make money online is a question I get asked quite a lot. In fact, it's probably the single biggest dream of those still trapped in dead-end corporate jobs. To the ill-informed, the internet represents a game-breaking new frontier for making money doing whatever you want. This is a very short-sighted belief and this type of 'get rich quick' mentality is what stops so many people from actually getting started on solid ground.

Despite the modern hype, doing business online is not fundamentally different than doing business offline. The internet simply offers a new, rapidly evolving venue to promote and operate your business on.

What the internet is NOT:

- A magic button for generating cash for little or no work.
- A shortcut or substitute for building a real business model or creating real value.
- A passing fad for business.

- Something which requires a highly technical skill set that only geniuses and geeks can learn.

WEBSITES

Websites used to be very difficult and expensive to build. Now, there are platforms which will allow you to host and maintain a basic website for free, or a more dynamic one for a small monthly fee. Wix, Weebly, and Squarespace are some of the most popular simple website builders with drag-and-drop functionality for non-designers. WordPress is a popular content management system with greater freedom in design and function, but which is also more complicated to use. These, and other tools, make starting a professional-looking website very affordable and easy for most businesses.

Your website is simply an interactive representation of your business. At the very least, it should communicate the products/services you offer, the values you stand for, and a very easy way to begin buying from you. The most basic ones are essentially glorified business cards or brochures, with the sole purpose of getting a visitor to call or email you. A website can also be an entire portfolio of work, or a thriving e-commerce store with many product offerings, a shopping cart, and payment processing capabilities. When most people complain about building or designing a website, they are really complaining about not having a clear vision for what their business should look like.

Your website will need at least a small amount of written content and other media to make your business look like a legitimate professional entity they can trust. Many new entrepreneurs overthink this problem, wanting to capture the minutia of who they are and what they think makes their business so special. They also don't understand what a typical visitor is looking for when they click onto their site. The way people use the internet these days often gives you only a few seconds to capture interest and convince a visitor to keep reading.

The homepage of your website can be as simple as a single tagline and paragraph of exposition summarizing what your company does, what makes it unique, who it's for, and what you want the reader to do next. It can also go on much longer, detailing some of the values of the company and selling points of your flagship product to entice further reading. Depending on how much you have to say, you can expand your message on your About, Products/Services, FAQ, and other pages. You either need to spend enough time online to familiarize yourself with modern trends and practices or else pay someone with expertise in this area.

Internet marketing is about getting strangers to pay attention to you. That means you must go to where they are already spending their time and give them a compelling reason to divert their mind towards you. Even in the relatively young context of the internet, there are many ways to do this, and the opportunities continue to grow every year. Here are just a few categories to pay attention to.

PAID ADVERTISEMENTS

The most common forms of online paid advertisements include banners on websites, sponsored posts on social media, pre-video ads on YouTube, and so forth. They are most effective if you have a very short, clear message, and a very well-defined target demographic. You do not want to pay for a general advertisement displayed to completely random people in the hopes that a few of them will actually be enticed to click through to your site. That's a quick way to blow your advertising budget.

CONTENT MARKETING

Another way to get people's attention is by having something valuable that they will actively be looking for. Social media, blogging, podcasts, and YouTube channels are all very effective ways to organically grow a following through the production of valuable content. For the right personality types, this is an excellent strategy, but it does generally take a long time to see meaningful results.

COLD OUTREACH

The previous examples require waiting for someone to notice you. They can be considered passive or indirect ways of marketing. They are analogous to setting a trap, making it as appealing as possible, and hoping the right prey will wander into it. A more direct approach would be to go hunting, meaning to reach out to people where they aren't already looking for you. There is nothing stopping you from calling, emailing, sending physical mail, or even going door to door promoting your business to anyone who publicly lists their contact information.

Showing up out of the blue in someone's email inbox or on their phone is a daunting task for most people. They don't like the prospect of chasing a target down with spear in hand, relying only on their strength and wits to bring it down. With practice, you can learn how to present yourself in such a way that they will make even complete strangers want to keep talking to you. Then your outreach will be free, as you will see prospecting opportunities everywhere.

THIRD-PARTY PLATFORMS

You can use third-party platforms external to your website to advertise, build a reputation, and accept payments. Freelancing directories like Upwork, People Per Hour, Fiverr, and others like them have the advantage of already having cultivated a large qualified audience and will gladly put you in front of them for an upfront fee or a cut of what you charge. For physical products, e-commerce sites like Amazon and eBay are an excellent way to showcase what you have.

These can work extremely well, because people are already actively looking to spend money on them, and most of them allow you to build up feedback based on good transactions. The downside is that you are ultimately controlled by the policies of the sites you sell through, and they usually take a 10-20 per cent commission on everything you charge. That's a small price to pay though for a beginner with no following of his own to get started.

Want More?

Thank you for reading my book. I would really appreciate it if you could take a moment to post a review on Amazon. It only takes a moment of your time and helps me out a lot as a first-time author.

The themes of this book have been turned into an online course, which will guide you through the changes you need to make to hone in on your brand identity. You'll get detailed guidance from me as you work through a better way to talk to your audience.

www.brandidentitybreakthrough.com/course

I am also available to help your company find their identity, overhaul their sales processes, and speak or teach classes/workshops almost anywhere in the world. If you have a non-profit education group, please don't hesitate to ask how I can be of service to you and your members.

To inquire about working directly with me in a coaching or mentoring capacity for yourself or your business, please visit identitypublications.com and apply for a consultation. We will discuss your reasons for seeking identity guidance, what you expect to get out of it, and why you specifically chose me for this fundamental process of deep inner and outer work.

Acknowledgments

My deepest admiration goes out to Helena Lind, for having seen who I am before even having met me. Her perspective as a fellow hunter and aspiring superhero has been invaluable to the development of my burgeoning brand identity.

There were many brave souls who volunteered their time to critique early drafts of this book, conservatively doubling or tripling the quality of the work. Among them were Sarah Schaetti, Anna Downes, Jeanine Leder, Robert Heider, Joe Lev, Philip Higginson, Nathan Rose, Janez Trobevzek, Rebecca Cable and Tim Coulter.

Finally, I would like to once again honour the late John Pugsley and our mutual associates for intervening at a critical avenue in my life. The ideological thought seeds planted years ago have grown into new structures for living, and I continue to pass his principles on through my actions and my words every day. The works of his lifetime continue to be relevant in a rapidly changing political and economic landscape because he thought and wrote in principles—a noble trait which I have aspired to emulate.